Rún Valdr
Rune Power/Authority

Rún Valdr

Rune Power/Authority

Rodney Cox

Rún Valdr Publishing 2017

First Printing: 2017

ISBN 978-0-9986907-0-4

Rún Valdre Publishing

All illustrations, symbols, photos, and figures by Rodney Cox

http://www.uberrod.com/runvaldr01.html

Dedicated to my lovely wife, Liz. Also to my Gods Odin and Freyja, without whom this work would not be possible.

Contents

1

Chapter One
Introduction

This book describes an independent energetic magical system. It should be noted that much of the information presented in this book comes from information gathered in trance journey work. This can also be called unverified personal gnosis (UPG). This is particularly true with the Rún Valdr specific symbols, received from the God and Goddess, Odin and Freyja, as well as the information on magical theory presented in Chapter Six. While I have made reference to lore as needed, especially in the section covering the runes, the bulk of this work is not directly from Norse lore.

However, this in no way diminishes the value of Rún Valdr. The real test of any system is whether or not it works, and Rún Valdr does indeed work.

What is Rún Valdr?

Rún Valdr (pronounced: Roon-Vahld-er) is a system of using and manipulating energy by means of attunements and symbols. What does this mean? It means that by getting a specific attunement, one can gain the ability to access and channel some form of "universal" energy through one's body for a variety of purposes using Norse runes and other symbols. This system can be used for healing, meditation, magic, and even religious purposes, to name a few.

Rún Valdr may seem very similar to the energetic healing system known as Reiki. While Rún Valdr shares some specific similarities to Reiki, there are a number of fundamental differences. To be very clear, Rún Valdr is completely separate and independent from Reiki. It is not a different flavor of Reiki, nor is it based on Reiki at all. It merely shares some Reiki-like characteristics. To repeat, it is not Reiki.

Given the number of similarities, there must be some comparisons made to Reiki throughout this book. Since this is not a book on Reiki, not a lot of time will be spent discussing or describing Reiki specifically. You may find more information on Reiki in the many books and/or online resources available if you are interested.

Characteristics of Rún Valdr

At a basic level Rún Valdr is an energetic system of power, or magic. It is not limited to just healing and the practitioner is free to use it for any purpose they choose. First and foremost, Rún Valdr is a magical system.

The characteristics of Rún Valdr can be broken down in these following points.

1. One must receive an attunement in order to use Rún Valdr.
2. The system is energy based.
3. You don't use your own energy.
4. The system makes use of many symbols, which includes the Norse runes.

5. The practitioner is in total control of the energy and directs the energy during a working.
6. Concentration must be maintained on the energy flow during a working.
7. Rún Valdr is especially good for creating magical objects.
8. Rún Valdr offers a variety of useful magical tools.

We will look at each of these characteristics in turn.

One must receive an attunement in order to use Rún Valdr

Before one can use Rún Valdr, one must be attuned to the specific Rún Valdr energy, and to the symbols that are used in the system. Rún Valdr uses attunements to pass on the ability to work with this energy and the various symbols. This attunement is an initiation that changes the recipient, allowing them to tap into the Rún Valdr energy. In other words, there is no Rún Valdr without undergoing an attunement process. However, the attunement is not very long or complicated. It takes only a matter of minutes for the attunement to be done.

The attunement can only be done by someone who is already attuned to Rún Valdr. Rún Valdr is passed from one practitioner to the next. The attunement process will be discussed in Chapter Five and is very different from any Reiki attunements.

The system is energy based

Rún Valdr allows one to make use of energy that is channeled through one's body. It is not based on herbs, or crystals, or stones or other physical methods. It relies on purely energetic sources to accomplish one's goals. It must be recognized that a purely energy based method has its advantages and disadvantages. It has the advantage of quickness and versatility, but it may take more time for the working to manifest.

You don't use your own energy

This concept provides a great advantage in energy work. In Rún Valdr, since you tap into an external energy source, you don't have to rely on your own energy, which is finite. You don't need to worry about running out of energy. Not being tied to your own energy allows you to do more and opens the door to greater work. The biggest goal then is to become a better conduit so that the energy can be channeled with greater ease and with an increased amount of energy flow. Simply put, the more energy you can channel, the more you can do.

The system makes use of many symbols, which includes the Norse runes

Rún Valdr makes use of the Norse runes and also unique symbols that are used during a working. These symbols help to guide and focus the energy to meet your needs and desires for the working. Your house is filled with electricity, and this electricity can be thought of as the raw Rún Valdr energy. By itself it is powerful, but unfocused. But run it through a toaster and you get toasted bread, a television and you can watch programs, lightbulbs, and you can light up a room. The symbols are like the devices you use that run on electricity. Different symbols/runes produce different results.

The runes will be discussed in Chapter Two, and the Rún Valdr specific symbols in Chapter Three.

The practitioner is in total control of the energy and direct directs the energy during a working

In Reiki, it is recognized that the Reiki energy is intelligent, dedicated to healing only, and does what it thinks best, sometimes against the wishes of the healer. There are anecdotal stories of someone being worked on for a broken toe, but finding that a headache went away instead. In Rún Valdr, you are working with a more universal/generic type of energy. It is up to you to direct it to achieve the desired results. It will not do the work for you. You tell the energy where to go, and what to do to achieve the goal of the working.

Given your control, intention becomes very important. Many runes, and some symbols have more than one meaning or use. The particular aspect you are working with is determined by your intensions. Because of this one must be clear on one's intentions as this system may be used to harm as well as heal, or to create. It does not have inherent safeguards to keep it from being abused.

More specific instruction on using the Rún Valdr system will be covered in Chapter Four.

Concentration must be maintained on the energy flow during a workings

One of the drawbacks of the previous characteristic is that while you are in total control of the energy, if you lose concentration on what you are doing, you will lose the connection of the energy. When this happens you will have to start over again. Rún Valdr is not a fire-and-forget solution. If you are exhausted, for example, it may be hard to properly use the system.

Rún Valdr is especially good for creating magical objects

Rún Valdr offers a method of creating self-powered magical items that is easy and quick. One essentially attunes an object and links it to a power source, such as the sun or the Earth. The object then becomes constantly filled with energy from this source. The applications for this are limitless. Instructions for creating magical items with Rún Valdr will be covered in Chapter Seven.

Rún Valdr offers a variety of useful magical tools

There are symbols that can bridge time and space, which is useful for targeting spell workings. The energy conduit symbols can send energy from a source of your choosing into a working, or item. There are symbols for resonance and authority which are invaluable in magical work. More information on magical theory will be covered in Chapter Six

Chapter Two

Runes

Since the heart of Rún Valdr is the runes and symbols we will take some time to explore runes in this chapter, and the Rún Valdr specific symbols in the next. While the symbols of Rún Valdr are fairly straightforward, runes have multiple meanings and associations. It is these differing layers of meaning that make runes so fascinating and useful. However, because each rune has several different associations attached to them (some of them seemingly contradictory) it is important to keep one's intentions clear on what aspect you are working with. As mentioned before, intentions play an important part in using Rún Valdr symbols and especially so when using runes.

The runes have a long history and many books have been written about them. We will not spend a great amount of time on the history of runes as there are so many other sources of information available. There will be some history, but for the most part, the bulk of the chapter will give an over view of each rune and how it applies to Rún Valdr. For more detailed information a list of rune books will be provided in the Appendices.

First, a brief history of the runes. They were used from the 2nd to 18th centuries, although after the Germanic areas became Christianized, the Roman alphabet was largely adopted and rune use for writing dwindled greatly. Regarding how the runes were developed, R.I Page says it best in *Reading the Past, Runes*,

"Where and when runes were invented we do not know. The obvious similarities with the Roman alphabet brought early scholars to the belief that the script appeared first among Germanic peoples within or close to the Roman Empire, with the implication that runes were an adaptation of the more prestigious alphabet for barbarian purposes."

Page then mentions other theories, such as that the runes were developed by Romanized Germani in what is now southern Switzerland and northern Italy. He also mentions evidence that runes may have been developed in Eastern Europe. And finally that runes may have been developed in Denmark. Dr. Jackson Crawford in his web videos suggests that the runes were derived from the Greek alphabet. Despite all the theories, we really do not know precisely when or where the runes were developed.

Regarding runes being used for divination, there are three sources that talk about this. The first is from Tacitus' *Germania* where it is noted that slips of wood had symbols written on them and then they are pulled at random as part of a divination system. It is not clear if this described actual rune use or some other symbol system. The second is from the Ynglinga saga where a king goes to Uppsala for a blot and the "chips" fell in a way that told him he would not live long. The third source is Rimbert's *Vita Ansgari*, where three accounts of drawing lots is mentioned. Nowhere is in specified that runes were being used. Even Jane Sibley, who is devoted to primary sources, couldn't come up with any new lore beyond these three. Yet she was able to contact people in remote rural areas of Scandinavia where runic divinatory practices have survived. It is my opinion that most divination practices are modern. That said, doing divinations can help one learn the meanings of the runes and help make them a part of your daily life and is a recommended practice.

Runes were written on many objects and usually identified the rune maker, or the owner of the item such as weapons and jewelry. Some were carved into monument markers to honor a person, such as a husband or wife or brother who had died. Others were obviously used for magical purposes and many weapons were inscribed with runes most likely to aid in battle. Jane Sibley in *The Divine Thunderbolt* lists a great number of weapons and other items with battle magic. One example is a fifth-century wooded spearshaft from a bog in Kragehul, Denmark. It has a runic inscription that reads "I, Asugisalas' erilaR, Muha am called. Go! Go! Go! The cosmically/magically-powerful-sacred hail [I] hallow/bless with/as [this] s[pear]". Also the Kowel spearhead has (in runes) the word Tilarids, which could possible mean "target-seeker" which is perhaps the weapons name.

R.I. Page notes that from the shape of the runes and the fact that there are no horizontal lines at all, one can come to the conclusion that the earliest use was on wood and thus all the lines carved went against the grain. If lines went with the grain it would increase the likelihood of the wood splitting. If the earliest use was on wood, it would not have lasted very long compared with the other medium that was used and would explain why there are very few examples of wood carved runes.

Runes were found in several different sets or Futharks. The name Futhark is derived from the first six letters of the rune set. F, U, TH, A, R, and K, similar to how the word "Alphabet" is derived from the first two letters of the Greek alphabet, Alpha and Beta. The most well-known are the Elder Futhark, the Anglo-Saxon Futhork and the Younger Futhark. Of course, variations of the Futhark are found throughout Scandinavia and are not limited to Norway or parts of England. There are Danish, Frisian, and Swedish runes, to name a few.

The rune set that is favored for Rún Valdr is the Elder Futhark. They certainly have a mystique about them, plus there are more runes than in the Younger Futhark. However, if the reader prefers some other rune set they are free to use them. The earliest listing of this entire Futhark set is seen in the fifth and early sixth century CE. This consists of three rows of eight runes each for a total of 24 runes. The Elder Futhark can also be seen listed out in one long row, such as the inscription on the Kylver Stone from around 400 CE (see below).

The Elder Futhark:

The Younger Futhark:

Much later in Norway (8th-9th centuries), during what is known as the "Viking Age" and other parts this was shortened to 16 runes and is called the Younger Futhark. The Younger Futhark is the rune set used during the Viking Age, and most of Old Norse was written using this rune system.

The Anglo-Saxon Futhork:

In England, the runes were expanded up to 33 runes. This is known as the Anglo-Saxon Futhork which would have been in use before the shift in the Norse language. In the Anglo-Saxon Futhork, the A sound had, over time, been modified to an O sound and that letter, Os stands for O rather than A. Which is why it's called a Futhork rather than a Futhark. But it retained much of the same esoteric associations as the Elder Futhark.

It should be noted that the Anglo-Saxon Futhork, is an older rune system than the Younger Futhark. A quick glance shows that it retains all of the runes from the Elder Futhark

There are other rune sets out there; Danish, Frisian, Swedish, etc. However to keep things simpler, we will focus on the Elder Futhark, the Younger Futhark, and the Anglo-Saxon Futhork because of the available rune poems.

Each rune row is called an aett (family) and is usually named after a God. Jane Sibley, in her self-published rune notes, mentions that they are named: Frey's Aett, Hagal's Aett, and Tyr's Aett. Kveldulf Gundarsson, in *Teutonic Magic*, names the first aett, Freyja's Aett.. Frey is the brother of Freyja and is a Vanic god, associated with fertility of the land, among other things. Tyr is the Aesir associated with justice and war. Paul Rhys Mountfort, refers to the fist aett as Frey's Aett, and that Hagal's Aett represents hail. Gundarsson also mentions that Hagal's Aett, is alternatively known as Heimdall's Aett. The only other reference to a Hagal that I have found is in the saga Helgakvitha Hundingsbana II, where the hero Hegi is fostered by King Hagal.

I have not seen any good explanation as to why, in the Elder Futhark, there are eight runes per row and three rows of characters. Nor is there seen much to explain the specific rune order. There are many examples of all the runes being written out and they invariably follow the same order. The only exception is the last two runes. Most inscriptions have Dagaz and Othala as the last two. However some have them reversed so that Dagaz is the last rune. Still, the earliest versions written out are just one long line of runes rather than being broken up into three rows, so maybe the three rows of eight is a fairly modern thing.

This is seen in the Kylver Stone inscription.

However, looking at the runes from a magical point of view the aetts become important. There are special codes used for writing runes, and in these codes the first and third aetts are often switched. But this magical usage could come from the time of the Younger Futhark and that the idea of three rows was then retroactively applied to the Elder Futhark.

There is much speculation for the rune order, from seeing it as a story of creation to seeing each aett as a specific area of human life, such as the first aett as cosmic concerns, the second as adversarial and the third as the human condition. It seems that much of this is mere speculation based on guesses. Some of it fairly well reasoned guesses, but still guesses. We may never know for certain.

The Kabalistic Tree of Life starting from the top and working towards the bottom tells a story of manifestation of the universe, from the nothingness of the beginning to the final result of the physical world. Some authors see the rune order as telling the same kind of story. It seems more believable that this is merely Kabalistic ideas being pushed onto the runes. After all, the Hebrew alphabet is assigned to the paths along the Tree of Life, which is also the basis of the major arcana of the tarot. It was probably too tempting not to look at runes in the same way, as a similar pathway of manifestation. It is more plausible, in my opinion, to accept that runes are magical just because in a society that is mostly illiterate, being able to read is magic. There is no reason to add extraneous systems on top of the lore already in existence. It does explain, however, why Edred Thorsson sees Fehu as the Cosmic Fires of Creation if it is the first rune with Othala, home, being the last.

Rune Books

It is helpful to read rune books with a grain of salt. Many authors come up with ever more elaborate and hidden meanings for each symbol. This is not to say that the runes are not complex, or that all rune authors are completely wrong, just that one should keep in mind that many of their interpretations may be quite modern and draw from material not necessarily related to early rune lore. For example, authors have pulled ideas from ceremonial magic, theosophy, yoga and other places that have no clear connection with runic studies in and of themselves.

Authors to avoid are those who seem to be making things up because it sounds cool or show a lack of understanding on the origins for the runes. Granted without some experience, this can be hard to figure out. Any author that talks about the "blank" rune should not be trusted as a rule of thumb. In a magical or divination system based on any ancient alphabet, a blank letter has no meaning. Also the idea of the blank rune was created solely by Ralph Blum and has no acknowledgement in lore. Most likely, the blank rune was an extra one in case you lost a rune, you could re-create it. Some authors try to blend runes with other systems such as the Kabalah or other systems far removed from the ancient Norse, like Native American spirituality. These attempts never mesh well. It fails because you are essentially trying to fit a square peg into a round hole. Runes have a specific history and lore built over the centuries. Throwing together ideas from completely different cultures and viewpoints will be problematic at best. One can understand a desire to create a comprehensive set of correspondences for everything, but sometimes it's better to look at various systems as standalone concepts rather than trying to force them together.

This leads to one of the greatest blunders, in my opinion; that of assigning runes to the major arcana of the tarot. Not only do you have the difference of 24 runes and 22 major arcana/paths, authors seem to have odd pairings of runes and major arcana. Rarely is Uruz used for Strength even though the main concept of this rune is physical strength. The Tower is defined as destruction that leads to something better, which describes Hagalaz perfectly, but these two are rarely matched up. And what to do with the extra runes? Where do you put them? Either they are left out, or one card will have multiple runes arbitrarily attached to it. Then there are major arcana that do not have any correlation to the runes and vice versa. Judgment comes to mind or Thurisaz or Dagaz. As mentioned above it is mostly trying to fit square pegs into round holes and the results are never as good as if you treated each system separately. If you find yourself reading books that do this, please do not accept anything written at face value. Do your own research to validate the material for yourself. This goes for my interpretations as well

There are lots of books about runes on the market. Here are some ideas to distinguish better authors from those with little historical lore knowledge. One should look for authors that draw as much as possible from primary sources, including the various rune poems. And if they do speculate, they can show a certain amount of logic behind what they are saying. One should migrate towards authors such as Jane Sibley, who focuses on primary sources, and away from authors like Edred Thorsson, who brings in concepts from other non-rune systems.

Now is a good place to discuss unverified personal gnosis (UPG) in more depth. This is ideas and concepts that come to people while meditating, praying, working with divination tools, etc. that are not found in written lore, but seems to ring true for them. To give an example: Say John, while doing trance journey work to visit Thor, always sees Him wearing a gold nose ring. Thor tells John (while in trance), that it represents Thor's ability to bring prosperity. This sounds really great, however, you will not find any lore with a description of Thor with a gold nose ring. This is some new bit of knowledge that only John is aware of. Is John wrong? Is he right? Well, that depends.

The tricky part of UPG is that it may be true, or it could just be the wishful imaginings of John. If John is the only one seeing Thor with a gold nose ring than it could all just be in John's head. Or, it could just be how John's subconscious interprets an expression of Thor's role in bringing prosperity. Maybe John just has a thing for nose rings. However, if multiple people independently start seeing Thor with a gold nose ring, then John's idea gains more merit. Or if someone is given a magical technique that is not covered in lore, but it works, that is also verification.

It is vital, that authors clearly state when they are offering readers UPG versus ideas and concepts taken directly from lore. It is freely admitted that the bulk of the Rún Valdr material is UPG. From the Rún Valdr symbols, to the techniques, to the magical theory found in Chapter 6, and everything in Chapter 8. However, Rún Valdr, as a system, works, which brings same validation in regards to this particular UPG. I won't say that the symbol Shai Nal is taken straight from runic lore, because it's not. Better authors will let the reader know which parts of their books are UPG.

The Rune Poems

If you want to look at primary sources for the runes you need to go to the rune poems themselves. There are several rune poems coming from Norway, Iceland and England that describe the properties of the runes. These poems are really the only primary source on the meanings of the runes. While it is nice to have a definitive source, there are problems with them as well that must be taken into account.

The main problem with the poems is that none of them describe the Elder Futhark rune set directly. Instead, they describe much later rune sets, the Anglo-Saxon Futhork (Anglo-Saxon poem) and the Younger Futhark (Norwegian and Icelandic poems). While these poems are not geared towards the earliest versions of the runes, they still have merit in attempting to glean meaning about the Elder Futhark set. All three rune poems will be included when discussing each rune where such a poem exists.

The next problem is that since these were written by Christians, and not Pagans, there is ambiguity that these actually represent the deeper, or magical meanings of the runes. They could merely be mnemonic devices to help remember the runes. Indeed, in the Abecedarium Nordimannicum, from the 9th century, you see such a mnemonic usage, "Feu first, Ur after, Thur is the third letter, Os is following it. etc." where no actual meaning is ascribed to the runes. How can we be sure that the rune poems we have to work with are not just some monks UPS? We can't. However, the poems are all we have to work with and we must set aside the problems and take the plunge.

Keep in mind that the Younger Futhark is a much later development and has fewer runes than the Elder Futhark so not all the Elder Futhark runes are covered by these poems. The Anglo-Saxon rune poems have the most complete account of the runes. Instead of shortening their rune list, like the Norse did, they actually expanded them. Both the Old Norse and Old Icelandic poems, however, tend to have similar meanings when compared with each other. This can lead to different interpretations from the corresponding verses of the Anglo-Saxon rune poem. But even the Anglo-Saxon changed the runes around as vowel sounds changed, so while very close, they are not an exact match for the Elder Futhark.

As mentioned, the different rune poems were written down well into the time that Scandinavia was Christianized, which took place between the 8th and 12th centuries. The poems have a cultural slant that may not be totally in line with the Pagan ancients. So while the rune poems are the primary work we have to use, they are by no means free of bias. That said, they do give a glimpse into the early associations of the runes. The poems are rather brief and are often vague but well worth the effort to figure out. The time tables taken primarily taken from Paul Tuitéan's *The Roots of Midgard*, state that the adoption of the Younger Futhark took place around 700CE and this is approximately the time the Anglo-Saxon rune poems were written (generally given as written in the 8th or 9th centuries). The Norse rune poem survived in a 17th copy of a destroyed 13th century work. This puts it somewhere in the 1200s as an origin. The Icelandic rune poem is a 15th century work. Thus the Anglo-Saxon poems are the oldest and written at the time when in Scandinavia the language was shifting from Proto-Norse to Old Norse. This is followed by the Norwegian poem with the Icelandic being the youngest. However, all can be said to have been written down after the various areas were Christianized.

Both the Norwegian and Icelandic poems give much the same meanings and seem to give identical interpretations in most cases. Thus they can be used in conjunction to give a better overall meaning for each rune. The Anglo-Saxon rune poem is useful in that it covers all the Elder Futhark runes, unlike the other two poems. I find it frustrating to consider that the Norwegian and Icelandic poems describe a totally different rune system that may have only a passing similarity to the earlier Elder Futhark. It is kind of like using rock and roll songs from the present to interpret how music from the 1950s may have sounded. Dated much later, it can be argued that the basic meanings of the Younger Futhark, when compared to the Elder Futhark, had shifted as much as the alphabet itself that reduced the 24 earlier runes to 16. It would be wonderful to have a set of ancient rune poems directly related to the Elder Futhark, but we must work with the poems currently known.

This strange mix of Anglo-Saxon rune poem (Futhork), and the Norwegian/Icelandic rune poems (Younger Futhark) makes it awkward to try to find a definitive meaning for the earlier Elder Futhark. It leaves a lot of guess-work of meanings to try to make them fit and in many ways you have a round peg/square hole situation again, which leads to cherry-picking of ideas. The written material we have to work with is much later. The meanings of each sent both the Younger and the Elder, may well have radically shifted over time. This potential shift leads us to a less than ideal situation when interpreting the runes. For example the Anglo-Saxon poem for Uruz mentions aurochs, the Norwegian and Icelandic do not and seem inclined to talk about rain instead. Most authors just talk about the aurochs and ignore the later versions. Kenaz of the Anglo-Saxon and Kaun from the Norwegian and Icelandic have completely contradictory and seemingly unrelated meanings. Again, most authors stick with the Anglo-Saxon version and skip over the "ulcer" versions. Or they awkwardly try to fit in the ulcer aspect with the torch aspect. However with Ansuz, most authors go with the Norwegian/Icelandic association with Odin and give cursory nod to the communication/speech meaning of the Anglo-Saxon poem. Granted the Anglo-Saxon rune is more of an "o" letter rather that the "a" found in the Elder Futhark or the later Younger Futhark. This means that the Anglo-Saxon fourth rune does not represent the same letter as the fourth rune of the Younger Futhark and creates a wider gap in meanings.

What this means is that we cannot look to any of the rune poems as a definitive, or correct meaning of the Elder Futhark as they are too far removed from the original source. Personally I tend to view them as describing various aspects of the runes that may have been more popular at the time they were written down.

The ancient Norse loved what they called "kennings." These were poetic ways of describing things, i.e Delling's Door would be the dawn, or a wolf in the woods might be an outlaw human. When looking at the various rune poems keep in mind that it may be best not to take them too literally. Some of the more obscure references that at first glance seem to have nothing to do with the rune may be a kenning for something that does. An example from the Icelandic rune poem for Fé (Fehu): "(Wealth) = source of discord among kinsmen, and the fire of the floodplain, and the path of the serpent." Fire of the sea and the path of the serpent is obviously a kenning. Instead of thinking that this rune has something to do with fire or snakes, consider that one pans for gold, which is fiery bright, in rivers, which have floodplains, and also look like the curving path a serpent might take. This then brings the meaning back to gold/money, and wealth. The reason I bring up the idea of kennings is that it is essential to understand the concept when trying to interpret the rune poems. Otherwise, taking the rune poems at face value can cause misinterpretations.

I want to state that I am using the rune names listed in R.I. Page's book *Runes* from the Reading the Past series, with some small variations. The names are Germanic in origin, and it should be recognized that the Norse names as well as the Anglo-Saxon names are different. For example the first rune, Fehu is called Fé in the Norse version and Feoh in the Anglo-Saxon. For this book, I am using the Dickens translation for all three rune poems.

Finally I must say that I'm not a big fan of reversed meanings of runes. For example, if one were doing a divination and pulled a rune that is upside down one could see this as being the representing the negative aspects of the rune. While I will not overly discourage folks from using this method, I will state that I do not find it useful, especially when dealing with magical uses of runes. If drawing a rune upside down made it negative, then bind runes would be almost useless and some of the Younger Futhark runes are upside down versions of runes found in the Elder Futhark. This would mean that they would always have a negative meaning (unless they were themselves reversed). I will let the reader make up their own minds about it, but the official policy in Rún Valdr is that there are no reversed runes. But then, with how Rún Valdr works one really doesn't have to worry about reversed runes at all, so this really is a moot point outside of the realm of divination.

But reversed meanings or no, many authors hold that the runes can be used for good (weal) or for harm (woe) For example for Fehu, an author might say that it can be used for weal by increasing one's wealth or prosperity, but may be used for woe by causing discord, even among family members. Thus each rune has built into it the capacity to help or hinder. Whether you differentiate this by the direction a rune falls during a reading, or by other runes next to it, or by in intuitive "feel" of the question at hand and what the rune is trying to say is of little importance. In Rún Valdr, as has been stated already, it is the intention that guides what aspect of the rune is to be used during a working. Isa may be used to stop or freeze a situation, but it can also act as a bridge between two places. The only difference is in the intent.

Runes - Freyja's (or Freyr's) Aett

Fehu - Money

Norwegian Rune Poem:
[wealth] is a source of discord among kinsmen
The wolf lives in the forest.

Icelandic Rune Poem:
[wealth] source of discord among kinsmen
and fire of the sea
and path of the serpent.

Anglo-Saxon Rune Poem:
[wealth] is a comfort to all men; yet must
every man bestow it freely,
If he wish to gain honor in the sight of the lord.

Fehu means money, cattle, wealth. It is the money rune. Some authors have expanded on this to see Fehu as a rune of increase in general. Thus you would use it with other runes to increase their effectiveness. Because of this using Fehu and Uruz together makes for a good basic healing combination.

A key aspect of wealth in ancient Norse society was that it needed to be kept circulating to be healthy. In tales where dragons have hoarded gold, the gold is usually seen as cursed. Because it was merely hoarded and not used, it became stagnant and went bad. A measure of one's wealth in ancient Norse society was how much you could give out to your followers, or the community, thus the line about bestowing it freely in the Anglo-Saxon poem.

I will say that there are three runes that mean wealth. Fehu, which is mobile wealth, Jera, which is the fruitful year, when work is done to capture the abundance of the land, and Othala which is hereditary possessions, the wealth of the ancestors, as it were.

The various rune poems all agree that this rune is about money, but they caution that it should be freely given if the person wants approval. The Norse and Icelandic poems warn that money can cause strife among kin folk. Even in modern times, money trouble can cause marriages to fall apart and friends to become enemies. I wonder if the phrase, "The wolf lives in the forest," is a kenning for an outlaw who has been forced out of society perhaps because of thievery or other problems stemming from wealth (or lack thereof).

From the very basic and simple meaning of cattle, most authors quickly point out that cattle were the mobile wealth of the ancient people and the true mark of prosperity. From there they start talking about the fiery nature of the rune because kennings of "gold" often have fire in it, such as creek-fire. Fire then leads to increase in general, because in ceremonial magic fire represents expansion, and then things get fairly abstract in a hurry. For example in *Teutonic Magic*, Gundarsson mentions that Fehu governs the transfer of energy and can be used for drawing energy into oneself or projecting outwards. Also that it can be used to increase one's own power. This is quite a leap from the initial meaning of "cattle." As is the aforementioned Edred Thorsson's assertion that Fehu represents the Cosmic Fires of Creation.

Granted a cow plays a huge part in the Norse creation story where a cow, Audumla, comes into being between the powers of ice and fire. She then gives milk to the other life that is being created. That, along with the misunderstanding of the "fire of the sea/floodplain" line, I can see where some may make this speculative leap.

I supposed that, looking at cattle from a historical perspective, that if cattle meant wealth, then more cattle meant greater prosperity which could then be spread around for the betterment of the whole community. For woe, this would indicate either poverty or greed and miserliness which keeps wealth out of the system causing the community to suffer. I have already mentioned the idea that gold from a dragon's hoard was seen a cursed or spoiled. The old Norse people were big believers in keeping wealth circulating as the most healthy way to deal with money. One can apply this to the economy in general where it is always seen as being healthier when people are out spending their money and thus driving further growth. When people stop spending we end up with recessions and depressions. So I can see where Fehu can be thought of as a rune of increase.

We also know that circulating wealth was important to ancient Norse culture and if this circulation was not maintained then strife would occur. One can see from the sagas that the ancient Norse were very conscious of their own worth and getting what they think they were due. If a Norseman felt he was being denied what he knew was owed to him, then he would do what was necessary, even using violent methods, to right this wrong. We could look a bit deeper into this importance of mobile wealth and see it as the necessary of a flow of energy and the dangers of stagnation. Both the Norwegian and Icelandic poems talk about how money can cause strife among kinsmen. I see the part of the Old Norwegian poem about the Wolf lives in the forest as a kenning for outlaws. Outlaws would prey on people to rob them. Also being an outlaw meant that one was outside of the normal social order. They were cut off from help and prosperity. Thus we see the more negative aspect of wealth; or more precisely the lack of wealth.

The Anglo-Saxon poem talks about how wealth should be given freely. What can we glean from this? Well a healthy economics is based on people spending. I go out and buy goods from company X, who hires people to make product X and purchases raw materials from company Y, etc. Excessive saving leads to a decline in the economy. We can see this today. People got too far in debt for their own good, although the spending was initially good for the economy. Now they are forced to deal with this debt by saving and spending money on debt management rather than on goods and services. Thus there is a severe decline in the economy. To be rich in the ancient Norse culture was to be able to give away lots of wealth.

As Odin says in the Havamal:

> *Better not to ask than to over-pledge*
> *As a gift that demands a gift*
> *Better not to send than to slay too many.*

This can be seen as a statement of not spending too much, or getting into too much debt, if we apply it to personal finance.

Thorsson speaks of Fehu being associated with fire including the great cosmic fire of creation. One author, Gundarsson, echoes this sentiment and bases his idea on the Old Icelandic rune poem.

> [Money] is the [cause of] strife among kinsmen,
> and the fire of the flood-tide,
> and the path of the serpent.

I see this more as a kenning for gold rather than a literal association with fire or serpents. I feel that gold being called the fire of the flood tide means that it is shiny and shows up in a creek pretty easily and really doesn't have much to do with fire in and of itself. The path of the serpent could easily be a kenning for a river or river bed as they tend to look like the curved bodies of snakes.

I see Fehu as not just money, but related to good money management. We put money in banks who then take it and loan to others while we collect dividends, thus increasing our wealth while at the same time spurring on economic growth. It relates to making investments. We invest a bit, perhaps in a stock, then if it grows, we can sell it for a profit. Invest in seeds and they grow to produce many, many more seeds than what you started with.

Personally, I see Fehu as primarily a money rune and secondarily as a rune of increase. I normally don't go much further than that, mostly because I don't have to.

My reasoning for the idea that Fehu is a rune of increase comes from the Icelandic Saga of Egil Skallagrimssonar. The tale mentions that he stops at a dwelling where a young woman is sick. Someone had tried to do rune magic to make her better, but she only got worse. Egil saw the runes, written on whalebone, scraped them into a fire and then burned the whalebone. He spoke a verse;

> *No man should carve runes*
> *Unless he can read them well;*
> *Many a man goes astray*
> *around those dark letters.*
> *On the whalebone I saw*
> *Ten secret letters carved,*
> *From them the linden tree [woman]*
> *Took her long harm.*

Egil then carved new runes and placed them under the pillow. The woman got better immediately. Some authors have suggested that he carved nine marks instead of ten, but the translation I'm using does not give a specific number. How does this tie into Fehu? Well, there were many secret codes, discussed by Jane Sibley and Edred Thorsson, used for runes, such as the tree code, where you have a vertical line and any horizontal lines on the left side represented the rune aett and any lines on the right side represented the rune position. Thus a tree with two lines on the left and seven on the right would represent the second aett and the seventh rune, which is Algiz. Another code used simple vertical lines. Longer lines were the aett and shorter lines were the individual rune position. The line of the verse that mentioned secret letters could indicate that some sort of code was being used.

Now when working magic, it was also common to switch the first and third aetts. This is mentioned by Jane Sibley in her *Notes on Rune use, Norse Traditional Magic and Runic Divination* manuscript, and also mentioned by Edred Thorsson in *Futhark.* So the ten marks made by the failed runester could be interpreted as third aett, first rune and third aett third rune. If the first and third aetts were switched then this would be Fehu and Thurisaz. Thurisaz in rune poems has been called the "sickness of women." Thus Fehu increased the woeful aspect of Thurisaz. Now if Egil made nine lines he would end up with Fehu and Uruz. Thus if Uruz represents health/strength, Fehu in this case increased the weal aspect of Uruz causing the woman to get better. I have used Fehu and Uruz together as a general healing combination and it works great.

To sum up, Fehu is a rune related to money. If you need help with finances, or money, or possibly even a job, this is a good rune to use. I also see it as a rune of increase in that if you apply the concepts of keeping things circulating and proper investment, then it can increase the effectiveness of other runes.

Uruz - Strength

The Anglo-Saxon Rune poem says:

[Aurochs] is fearless
and greatly horned
a very fierce beast,
it fights with its horns,
a famous roamer of the moor
it is a courageous animal.

The Old Norwegian Rune poem says:

[Slag] is from bad iron;
oft runs the reindeer on the hard snow.

The Old Icelandic Rune poem says:

[Drizzle] is the weeping of clouds,
and the diminisher of the rim of ice,
(some versions say "and ruin of the hay-harvest")
and [an object for] the herdsman's hate.

Uruz means an auroch. Aurochs were a species of wild cattle that is now extinct. The last known auroch was killed in Poland in 1627. Aurochs were dangerous and aggressive animals. There are stories, from Caesar, of manhood rites where a young man would have to kill one to prove himself. The general meaning of this rune is strength and health as in the vital, primal strength of the animal that is associated with it. There are also associations with drizzle or rain which is based on rune poems. Again, one can look at the previous rune and the importance of circulation. If keeping money circulating is good for the economy, then keeping things in the body circulating is good as well. Blood, breath, water, etc all need to be kept moving or we die. Then we would also become stagnant and bad as well.

Jane Sibley sees Uruz as physical power operating in the physical world. Thus it could be seen to focus effort and work of a mundane or physical nature. If we keep with the health association one thinks of physical therapy, or perhaps physical exercise.

Uruz is another rune that seems open to a wide variety of interpretations. Some rune poems call it slag, others Aurochs, others drizzle. There seems to be no true unifying idea especially between the Icelandic and Norwegian poems. However, The Old Norse word for this rune úr (dross, or slag), is similar to another word úrr, which means "aurochs." There is another word ýr that means "bad iron" or "female aurochs", and ýrr means "mad, furious, wild". It is possible with shifting sounds, and spellings, that when it came time to write down the Norwegian and Icelandic poems, it seems that it was talking about rain/drizzle rather than aurochs. Reindeer could be seen as another word to describe an antlered beast. If you take the Norwegian and Icelandic poems as kenning for an auroch running wild through one's crops, they could be seen as a metaphorical storm trampling the crops (ruin of the hay-harvest), and makes this rune poem easier to understand.

Thus the Norwegian poem could be interpreted as

Ferocity comes from a female aurochs.
oft runs the antlered beast on the hard snow.

And the Icelandic poem could read,

Aurochs is the weeping of clouds
and the ruin of the hay-harvest
and [an object for] the herdsman's hate

But looking at the poems as we have them today, we can come up with other interpretations. While one of these poems talks about the auroch, mentioning its strength and might, the others deal with completely different imagery. The Old Icelandic poem talks about drizzle or rain and one version talks about the diminishing of ice. The Old Norwegian poem talks about slag and reindeer running on hard snow. All three mention movement; an auroch roaming the moor, rain or drizzle falling, and reindeer running. Slag coming from bad iron is about purifying. And the rain diminishes ice which can be seen as a blockage of movement or of stagnation. It's possible that the reference to the reindeer is some form of kenning. Most authors zero in on the auroch angle and ignore the rain reference. Some authors talk about how this rune represents the flow of water, and this flow can be seen as an important thing. Running water is cleaner than stagnant. This can be extended to our blood and breath and again shows the value of proper circulation. If we stop the circulation of either of these two things, we will die. Kveldulf Gundarsson mentions how Laguz is the water, Peorth is the well the water comes from, and Uruz is the flow of the zwater.

This rune relates to the previous rune Fehu. Where Fehu represents domesticated cattle, and shows the importance of mobile wealth that is kept circulating, this rune represents wild cattle. But the idea of circulation is still important. Not in terms of economics, but in body functions.

Together these three poems seem to talk about purifying the self to get rid of weakness so that one will be filled with strength and vitality. This is one of the reasons I see Uruz as a healing rune. As I mentioned above, movement and circulation keeps one healthy. The rune poems kind of shows a pathway to health. Meeting opposition head on builds strength, which leads to health. Our bodies tend to follow the idea of "use it or lose it." If we exercise, we become strong. If we don't we get weaker. The same is true of our immune system. We need a certain amount of germs and bacteria for our defense systems to get their proper exercise and stay strong. So overall, I see Uruz as strength and health, a general vitality of body and spirit. Fehu combined with Uruz makes a good general healing combination. In any sort of healing I always start with the Fehu/Uruz combination. It can also be used in situations where you need strength in general, or to strengthen a working.

Thurisaz - Giants

Anglo-Saxon Rune Poem:

The Thorn is most sharp, an evil thing to
take a grip on, extremely grim for any
man who rests among them!

Old Norwegian Poem:

[Giant] causes anguish to women;
Misfortune makes few men cheerful.

Icelandic Poem:

[Giant] =torture of women
and cliff dweller
and husband of a Giantess.

This rune is perhaps the one rune with the most conflicting meanings. On one hand it is often seen as the most destructive rune. It represents the Thurses, Giants who fought against the Gods and Mankind. It represents absolute destruction. It can be a very hurtful rune and I would caution any who use it to keep their intentions very clear and do what you can to limit its use or it will run away with you. Thurisaz is primal and aggressive. I would say that its primary attribute is aggressiveness, pure and undiluted.

The Giants, who fought against our Gods and mankind should not automatically be seen as evil. Rather they should be seen as powerful forces that are untamed, which can be dangerous to people. Like a hurricane, while not an evil force, can cause untold devastation to the human world. By defeating the Giants, the Gods brought order and a situation where humans could flourish. Yet, Giant-kind had its own beauty, power and value. The God Freyr married a Giant, Thor's mother Jorð is a Giant, and her name means "earth". Odin learned wisdom and knowledge from Giants. However, the wildness and untamed majesty can be dangerous for mortals.

Thurisaz does have some positive aspects and can be associated with the god Thor, who is a great protector of Mankind and fought against the Jotuns and Giants. It can be seen as a representative of the principle "A good defense is a good offense." It can be used as a counter attack to break an incoming threat, much like anti-missile systems are designed to take out incoming missile attacks by hitting them with other missiles. It is aggressiveness being harnessed for protection, but it is still naked aggressiveness.

Jane Sibley sees Thurisaz as Divine energy working in the physical world, which doesn't sound all that bad to me. I can see this illustrated as lightning striking the ground, particularly crops. Sibley talks about this being seen as Thor engaging in marital relations with His wife Sif, who has crop (particularly wheat) associations. Either way lightning comes from the sky, the realm of the Gods and it strikes the ground, thus Divine acting in the physical world. In some cases, at least with lightning, the effects can be devastating. More of this can be seen in her book, *The Divine Thunderbolt*.

As you can see, none of the rune poems mention Thor at all. However, He was half Giant and this mixture of heritage gave Him the strength needed to fight the Giants. This is an important idea one finds in quite a few Indo-European cultures, that to fight an enemy, you needed to have similar qualities. The statement fighting fire with fire comes to mind. Lugh of the Irish culture was needed to fight the Fomor because He himself was half Fomor, and so on. This is even seen in the 1999 movie, The 13th Warrior, where Vikings dealing with an alien threat needed an alien (Arab) person to go with them. Thus they were fighting the unknown with their own unknown.

I could see this as a good rune to use to attack viral, bacterial and fungal infections or to work against cancers. I imagine that any sort of working where the immune system needs to be bolstered would respond to Thurisaz. However, since Thurisaz can easily be used for very destructive ends I will repeat that when one uses this rune they will need to have very clear intentions and limits for the rune.

Thurisaz is a good rune if one needs active defense, such as against things like cancer, or to push things when mere passivity isn't helping. If you need to break something whether physical or spiritual/psychic, this is the rune to use. Especially useful for breaking out of dated connections to people you don't want to be energetically connected to any longer.

This rune, above all the others needs to be used the most carefully. Since it represents the untamable wildness and power of the Giant folk it needs to be used in a very conscious and deliberate way or it will get away from your control. You will need to set very strict guidelines for the working of this rune and have very clear intentions.

Ansuz. - Communication/Gods

This is normally seen as the rune of communication and is associated with the Gods and with Odin in particular. In a way it contrasts nicely with the previous rune. Where with Thurisaz you have the malevolent Giants, here you have the mighty Gods who watch over mankind, who bring the Good Rains the nurture crops as opposed to hurricanes and tornados. Ansuz is translated as "God." Jane Sibley sees this rune as Divine Power operating in the Divine Realm, while more modern rune scholars take this rune to be associated with communication especially with oral communication. I feel that this belief came from the sound shift that happened with the Anglo-Saxon rune set. the A-sound shifted to an O-sound and the name changed from Ansuz to Ass (pronounced Azz) to "Os" which is often translated as "mouth". The A-rune then found a home near the end of the Anglo-Saxon rune set and was re-named Aesc, or ash, and was used for æ. Thus we have a case where the Anglo-Saxon rune is really not the same as the Elder Futhark, or the Younger Futhark runes at all. Thus the meanings may be inaccurate at best.

The Old English rune poem says:

God/Mouth is the chieftain
of all speech,
the mainstay of wisdom
and a comfort to the wise ones

Thus we can see the shift from the rune meaning a God to mouth, which is the chieftain of speech. There is still an emphasis on wisdom, which Odin was chief of.

The Icelandic rune poem says:

Ase = Odin is the olden-father
and Asgard's chieftain,
and the leader of Valhalla.

The Icelandic poem echoes the Norwegian:

[God] =aged Gaurtr
and prince of Asgard
and lord of Valhalla.

The Anglo-Saxon poem talks about speech as the mainstay of wisdom. This shows the age of the poem, and harkens back to when knowledge was passed on by the spoken word in the form of stories and poems told to listeners by storytellers and bards. It is clear that this is an interactive experience. Because of this Ansuz can be seen as a rune of learning, of education. A lot of education is still teachers explaining things to students by speaking the information. Students can ask questions, and get answers in return. The Anglo-Saxon poem really is an expression of this idea. It tells us speech can teach, and in learning, we gain wisdom. Communication is key to society and culture. With good communication, comes understanding, and with understanding people can work together.

The Norwegian and Icelandic poems focuses on the God Odin. One can infer that this rune has qualities that are associated with

Odin. Wisdom, poetic inspiration, mental acuity, wisdom, and knowledge. And in a time when only a few were literate, the spoken word was the medium of transferring knowledge and wisdom from one person to another. The qualities of Odin, wisdom and wise speech is seen across all three rune poems. If one wants to work with these qualities, then Ansuz is a good rune to use.

As a God of wisdom, Odin is about learning, and using that wisdom, in addition to His other aspects of battle, death, and other things. These poems focus on Odin's thirst for knowledge and wisdom, and the terrible ordeals he underwent to gain these things. If knowledge and wisdom were unimportant they would not be worth suffering for. Odin hung from Yggdrasil for nine days and nights to win knowledge of the runes. He gave up an eye for a drink of Mimir's Well, gaining great wisdom.

Representing Odin, and all Gods in general, Ansuz can be a path to the divine. It can bring a touch of the Gods to a working. Jane Sibley sees Ansuz as the Divine acting on the Divine plane. As such it can be useful when consecrating ritual tools, or even items to be used as offerings to the Gods.

For Rún Valdr I tend to see this rune as one of learning, study, and communication. This is the rune to use for learning things, or to gain access to the Gods. Of course, since Ansuz represents Odin, it can be used where you would like His influence to be, or in contacting Him for any reason.

Raidho - Travel/Movement

I think there is some misinterpretation of this rune. A lot of people seem to see it as representing a vehicle like a horse or a car, most likely because the rune poems all mention horses. But the rune is usually translated as "Riding." Some authors look at this rune and stress the horse thus relating it to the vehicle rather than the journey. I think this is a mistake. In my mind the poems all relate to travel, but not travel on foot. The main vehicle at the time was, of course, the horse. Thus Raidho is the rune of movement and travel and on a broader scope can be seen as the path we travel in life.

The Norwegian Rune poem says:

[Riding] is said to be the worst thing for horses;
Reginn forged the finest steel.

The Icelandic poem says:

[Riding] =joy of the horseman
and speedy journey
and toil of the steed.

And lastly the Anglo-Saxon poem says:

Riding seems easy to every warrior
while he is indoors and very courageous
to him who traverses the high-roads on
the back of a stout horse.

The Icelandic and Norwegian poems seem to sympathize with the horse as it does all the work while allowing the rider relative ease.

As the saying goes, riding a horse may not be much faster than walking but at the end of the day it's the horse that's tired and not you. The Anglo-Saxon poem takes a different take and looks at how much easier travel seems when one is sitting indoors safe and sound compared with the difficulties one can face when actually travelling. All the poems, however, stress the riding and traveling as the main points even though all three mention horses as the vehicle. Raidho, then, is the travel rune and can be used when you travel. It is good to use on one's car to insure that it can travel well and properly.

The Anglo-Saxon poem in particular, which talks about how easy the road looks when one is sitting safely indoors says a lot about this rune and presents a key to the deeper meaning. The fact that travel, whatever kind that may be, always has its hardships and toil. It is said that it is not the destination, but the journey that matters. How we face and deal with the trials of the journey shape and define our character. Someone untested sitting at home talking about a journey cannot compare with the person who dares the dangers of the road. It speaks of a certain seasoning that comes with traveling along the road of your life. You learn things as you travel to different places, your horizons are broadened and hopefully you become wiser. What road are you taking? Your actions and decisions are, in a way similar to choosing between branching paths of a road. To go right means the left path is closed. To choose to work for a promotion in company A means you can't get a job in company B. Our life paths are as fraught with as much hazard as any physical trip and it is a brave person who boldly journeys. This then is the rune of movement, sometimes physical movement such as walking or more abstract as walking one's life path. Use it if you seek your way in life.

Kenaz - Fire

In some ways this is a very hard rune to nail down a concise meaning. The rune poems are not consistent at all between the Norse, Icelandic and Anglo-Saxon versions.

Anglo-Saxon Rune Poem:

> *[The Torch] is known to every living man*
> *by its pale, bright flame; it always burns*
> *where princes sit within.*

Norwegian Rune Poem:

> *[Ulcer] is fatal to children; Death makes a*
> *corpse pale.*

Icelandic Rune Poem:

> *[Ulcer] = disease fatal to children*
> *and painful spot*
> *and abode of mortification*

Here again we have a similarity between the Norwegian and Icelandic poems that are at complete odds with the Anglo-Saxon poem. While the Anglo-Saxon talks about a torch which brings warmth and light to nobles in their houses, the other poems talk about ulcers which indicate a disease, fatal to children in particular. Obviously a huge shift took place by the time the Younger Futhark came about. Where many scholars see this rune as one of inspiration and even sexual desire (which seems to be a very modern interpretation given the text of the poems), the Norwegian and

Icelandic poems give much different meanings. It could almost be seen as the fire of fever brought on by a disease. I am inclined, in this case, to see it as a reference to disease instead.

The Anglo-Saxon name for this rune is Ken. We use the word ken to mean "to understand," and the word "kenning" which represents poetic metaphors, would suggest the rune dealt with ideas and perhaps inspiration, at least from the Anglo-Saxon point of view. A torch, much like comparing Fehu (domestic cattle) with Uruz (wild oxen), would suggest the taming of the wild power of fire for human use. Torches inside allow one to stay active after the sun goes down and the world gets dark. This added time could be spent in leisure dreaming up poetry or other writing and thus represents leisure time to refine culture and to be inspired by non survival types of needs. This I feel is the basis for Kenaz being seen as a rune of inspiration. While at the same time I'm convinced the sexual aspect has more to do with modern authors seeing "fire" associated with the rune and then trying to link it to "fires of desire."

Fire under control can then be extended to the fires of the hearth and also of the forge. Cooking and smithcrafting are but two examples of fire being controlled for the good of humanity. And of course, to step outside of the Norse culture for moment one could look at the Irish idea of the Fire in the Head, representing poetic inspiration.

While it is fairly easy to talk about fire, torches and the benefits of Kenaz, it is more difficult to try to reconcile the Anglo-Saxon Rune Poem with its counterparts (Kaun in Norwegian and

Icelandic). The Black plague would most likely have struck Europe by the time the Norwegian rune poem was written down and definitely have struck by the time the Icelandic rune poem was written down. The second major outbreak of the Black Plague in Europe (the first was in the sixth century) happened in 1347, and the Norwegian poem can be traced to the 1300s. Iceland was hit by plague in 1402 as well as 1494, each time wiping out half the Icelandic population. The Icelandic poem was written in the 1400s. Both the Norwegian and Icelandic rune poems seem to echo this tragedy for some reason instead of the Anglo-Saxon meaning. The Anglo-Saxon rune means torch. The Norwegian and Icelandic runes mean ulcer, something totally different.

Edred Thorsson has an idea related to the ulcer part that makes some sense in trying to reconcile the torch meaning with the ulcer meaning. Basically you have two sides of the same coin. The torch is the creating, shaping aspect. The ulcer is the destructive, dissolving quality that drives true creation. Creation and destruction are both necessary in order to help shape the world. A bar of iron can't exist the way it is if you want to turn it into a sword or a horse shoe. Fire can be a destroying force or one of creation in that you can burn down a house, or use it to cook food, or forge tools. Thus you see ceremonial magic concepts of solve et coagula be introduced. Dissolving and coagulation, primal alchemical principles.

Both the Norwegian and Icelandic poems directly relate to disease and the death of children and seem to have little to do with re-shaping, or destroying to bring about new forms, or even the destructive properties of fire. Even if you see disease as a purging type of fire that clears away, the name of the Younger Futhark rune is ulcer, which has no real association with fire or a torch. It is increasingly clear to me that by the time the Norwegian and Icelandic poems were written down this rune was associated with a virulent plague. The associations of the rune had shifted completely from torch (tamed fire) in the Anglo-Saxon to death and disease and sorrow in the Younger. If you were living in a time when there was great plague you would need a rune for any divination or magic related to disease. The bubonic plague left big sores that you can easily see as directly related to both the Norwegian and Icelandic poems when they mention "ulcer" or "painful spot." If you consider the need to burn bodies I can understand where the original meaning of torch could possibly shift to plague and death that ends up being put to the torch rather than the benefits of light in a dark place. A cleansing fire, if you will, rather than the fires of inspiration. Or perhaps the fires of fever. The Anglo-Saxon Futhork had a rune that meant death and destruction, Ear, so they wouldn't need to add one like the Younger Futhark did.

In the end I really cannot reconcile the two different meanings and would default to the Anglo-Saxon meaning as it is the older of the poems, and therefore closer to the original intent in my mind. The Norwegian and Icelandic seem to be a more modern interpretation and no are no longer connected at all to the Elder Futhark runes. Now if I were dealing strictly with the Younger Futhark then I would see this rune to mean death and suffering. But when looking at the Elder Futhark this meaning just doesn't fit in my opinion.

So to sum up, I would stick with the torch meaning. Tamed fire that is useful for human culture. Fire can be transformative and this rune can be used in the same way, to help shape events around us, or to shape our thoughts for creative output. It can light the way to new paths and thoughts and show us things we have never seen before.

Gebo - Gift

This is usually seen as a good rune. While appearing in the Elder Futhark and Anglo-Saxon Futhork, this rune does not appear in the Younger Futhark. The K letter, Kaun, would end up doing double duty. Thus, in terms of rune poems, we only have the Anglo-Saxon rune poem to look at.

> *[Generosity] brings credit and honor,*
> *which support one's dignity; It furnishes*
> *help and subsistence to all broken men*
> *who are devoid of aught else.*

This particular translation of the poem shows a wide variety of associations and a complexity of ideas. Generosity, giving gifts represents the idea of honor. The poem clearly states that generosity (giving of gifts) brings credit and honor which supports one's dignity. This was very important to the Norse. One never wanted to be seen as a miser, so when receiving a gift, you always gave more in return. By giving gifts or being generous you both earn a good name and thus increase one's honor and dignity. It also helps those less fortunate than yourself. This poem seems to focus more on charitable work than the Havamal which takes more formal stance where a gift demands a gift and stating that it is better to not give than to over give. To say a gift demands a gift leads to the idea of reciprocity, and to the social custom of hospitality, which was a key concept to the Indo-European peoples. Numerous stories and sagas show good hospitality being rewarded, and bad hospitality being punished. Reciprocity is also the basis for ADF's devotional pattern of making offerings and then receiving blessings in return.

We can look at the shape and see that it in entirely made up of chevrons and thus should be a very active rune (I'll discuss this at length later in the chapter). This can be seen in the idea of exchange and circulation of wealth and aid being important. It was not something that is passive or hoarded. Money had to be kept moving or it became stagnant. Same with relationships. You needed to maintain those by giving and receiving gifts and hospitality. You could not just sit doing nothing and expect it to flourish.

Some authors see this as a marriage rune and in some ways I can see this as valid. In a marriage there is a normal and constant give and take between the two people in the relationship. Both have to contribute to make it work. For either partner to take a passive role is to end up taking the other for granted. Because of this it is a social rune to be sure and forms the basis of all of our interactions with other people. It teaches how best to interact with others and sets a practical lesson for the sayings "Do unto others as you would have them do unto you," "what goes around comes around," and of course, "It takes two to tango." If I literally act well to you, why would you not act nice in return? This fosters friendships, love relationships and friendly diplomatic exchanges between countries. And in the case of polyamory relationships, this reciprocity becomes even more important.

Any negative aspect would be in not giving enough, giving too much or expecting too much in return. Thus having unrealistic expectations would tend to hamper the goodness of this rune. I mean if I gave you a horse and in return you have me a crude drawing of a horse, I would feel a bit cheated. At least give me a couple of goats and a cow.

So in a way this rune can be used to make sure that our efforts are well rewarded. However it would be imprudent to use this rune to try to get more than you deserve. I think it would backfire and you would end up losing more to make up for it. It's not what I would call winning the Lotto kind of rune. But rather it's getting the promotion in payment for your hard work. It's getting help when you need it in repayment for aid you may have offered. For negotiating a fair contract, and, of course, marriage. Think of it as the good karma rune.

This reminds me of an old tv show, Stingray, where a guy would help others and in repayment would expect a favor from them in return at some point in the future.

The importance of this rune cannot be overstressed. The proper functioning of our society and spiritual lives is dependent on the principles that make up this rune. No man is an island and nothing better expresses this idea than Gebo. The idea of reciprocity and a gift for a gift forms the religious basis of Ár nDraíocht Féin, and in that token, most of the ancient Indo-European religions. Offerings are made to the Kindreds and blessings are the bestowed upon us. This is the formula for forging lasting relationships, not only between other humans, but between the Kindreds as well.

Looking at the old sagas, especially those from Iceland you see this principle helping and hurting people. A king took offense at his host having more troops when he visited. This started a blood feud that lasted generations. There are plenty of stories of the hero feeling slighted and not getting what they feel they deserve and in many cases physically going to war over it.

Always keep in mind that this rune is a two way street. This rune can be used when giving gifts to insure that proper reciprocity is awarded. It can open up dialogue and relationships between people and groups. The giving of gifts is the doorway to hospitality and friendship. It can also help to insure that the generosity you do is noticed so that your good name may increase.

Wunjo - Joy

Wunjo is one rune that has no negative associations at all. It is a rune of happiness and joy as the rune poems attest.

Anglo-Saxon Rune Poem:

> *Joy is for one who knows little of woe,*
> *unhampered by sorrow he will have*
> *bright fruits and bliss and buildings*
> *enough.*

This is a happy rune. In the most basic sense this rune is quite simple. Joy, happiness. A lot of other authors seem to find this not enough and go off on, what I consider, wild tangents. Freyja Aswynn only talks about Odin and Ullr and how this rune relates to them, but never really stays with the joy part which is mentioned only in passing. Gundarsson talks about how it represents the will.

Sticking with the rune poem you really don't need to look beyond joy and bliss as an explanation, in my opinion. However you define it, this rune means happiness.

The last part seems to indicate joy in one's work in life. The ancient Norse were a hard working people and didn't care for laziness. So this joy would not be a life of leisure, but taking pride and joy in the work you do and in the life you are making for yourself. Perhaps this is why Gundarsson talks about Wunjo representing the will. If you apply yourself in a correct way you will prosper and be happy. He speaks not of the power of willpower where one grimly sticks to one's principles against all else, do or die. It is being mindful of your work and how you live your life so that when you are doing work you love your whole being is focused on the task. You are not divided on having to do something you hate and only do it half-heartedly. As the saying goes, "If you have a job you love, you won't work a day in your life." It won't be "work" it will be your vocation.

Not only is it about being happy with your work, the poem also suggests that it means being happy with what you have in life when it says, "he will have bright fruits and bliss and everything enough." Sometimes we get caught up in a mentality that the grass is always greened on the other side of the fence. Where everything else looks great, but what you have. While this sense of wanting more can inspire innovation and exploration, sometimes it just makes us miserable, even though we may have it pretty good. The poem teaches us that it is good to have enough, and to take joy in that.

This is a good rune to use if you are unhappy as everyone needs joy in their life. I feel it can help you see the beauty in life and to take pleasure in your everyday tasks. Everyone can use some joy. Combined with Raidho it can help you find that path in life that will lead to happiness. I would use it in cases of depression, sadness, or in overcoming grief.

Hagel's Aett

Hagalaz - Hail

Anglo-Saxon Rune Poem:

Hail is the whitest of grains. It whirls
from the sky whipped by the gusting
wind, then turns to water.

Norwegian Rune Poem:

[hail] is the coldest of grain; Christ
created the world of old.

Icelandic Rune Poem:

[hail] = cold grain
and shower of sleet
and sickness of serpents.

Hagalaz is the first rune of Hagal's Aet. As mentioned earlier there is not a lot of information on who or what Hagal is/was, but it could be that the aett is just named after the first rune, so it could be translated as Hail's aett, since the rune Hagalaz means hail. Jane Sibley takes the same interpretation and says it is named after hail.

This is an interesting rune in that it offers bad stuff and good stuff in the same rune. In fact the first three runes of this aett are normally what you call "negative" in meaning. Hagalaz is the disruption that clears the way for better things to come. Hail can damage crops, yet melt into life giving water. Fire brings renewal to a forest. The Jack Pine tree needs fire in order for its seeds to open and for the tree to propagate. I find it interesting that all three rune poems refer to Hagalaz as a "grain." I also wonder if the Norwegian poem is making mention of the creation story where the world eventually came into being by the union of fire and ice.

Hagalaz is disruption, which into every life must fall. It is never pleasant, but often is necessary. In the best light it is the clearing away of things holding you back so that you can make the next step, the next breakthrough, go to the next level. On a more negative level it is just disruption and there is nothing you can do about it. It is like swimming against the tide or current. You can try, but you won't have much to show for your efforts.

Jane Sibley likens it to lightning and talks about how this rune can be used in a protective manner. It is said lightning never strikes the same place twice. By using this rune you are saying, "Look, lightning has already struck here! No more woe can happen," and then misfortune moves on, not wanting to break the rules. As a protection method, this is quite different from Thurisaz which we have already discussed. Instead of "hit it first before it can hit us," Hagalaz is more sleight of hand and misdirection.

Some authors talk about how Hagalaz can represent taking action in response to tragedy and misfortune and point out how ambulances have the Younger Futhark version of Hagalaz painted on them. How we face disaster tells us about who we are rather than in the times when we are untested. Do we curl up and die, giving up? Or do we face those difficult times with steel in our backbones and iron in our will?

The big lesson with Hagalaz is that no matter how disruptive its influence is, something good will come of it. The hardship is not in vain. I gave a rune reading once and Hagalaz came up. The person's apartment building caught fire, but they ended up in a better place.

The Norwegian poem mentioning Christ creating the world is a bit puzzling and doesn't seem to fit. It does not seem to be a kenning, in my opinion. One can consider that ice was one of the original forces that led to the creation of the world, so perhaps, this is a reference to that. Or the person recording it randomly inserted the Christ reference to make up some space.

Use this rune when you need things shaken up or to get out of a rut. It can also be used for protection, as mentioned above.

Katie Gerrard in her book, Odin's Gateways, suggests that Hagalaz, Nauthiz and Isa represents winter. Hagalaz is the start of winter, Nauthiz is the middle of winter and Isa is the end of winter. Hagalaz is the first hail of winter, Nauthiz is the need of your stores to last through the dark, cold, winter. Isa is the last cold spell before winter ends. I do find this an interesting interpretation of these three runes although I don't necessarily see Isa in such a manner. If anything I would reverse Isa and Nauthiz where Isa is the depths of winter and Nauthiz is the need of new food when the stores run low at the end of winter.

Winter is a time of rest of renewal, but it must be prepared for. Hail can cause damage, but melts into water which gives life. Need teaches us to prepare for need and to take care of problems early. Ice can stop us or it can allow travel over water. Winter has its gifts, but they come at a price.

Still when using it magically, I can see it being good for getting one out of a rut, or for protection as Jane Sibley recommends. It could also be used to curse someone, bringing disruption. Because of the wide range of meanings, it is best (as with Thurisaz) to be very clear in your intentions and limitations on how the rune is to be used.

Nauthiz - Need

Like the rune before and the one after, this rune has some contradictory meanings although not as much as the other two. The rune poems illustrate this nicely.

Anglo-Saxon Rune Poem:

> *Need is a tight band on the breast, but it*
> *often can be turned into an omen of help,*
> *if attended to early.*

Norwegian Rune Poem:

> *[constraint] gives scant choice; A naked*
> *man is chilled by the frost.*

Icelandic Rune Poem:

> *[constraint] = grief of the bond-maid*
> *and state of oppression*
> *and toilsome work.*

Nauthiz can be a rune representing a state of need where you are in need of something you don't have. Whether this is needing medicine, stranded out on the highway with a flat tire, needing rent money, being stranded out on a glacier, loss of a loved one, or facing the destitution of homelessness, this rune can represent all that and more. Thus one could use this rune to put another into a state of need. To strip away what they have, to throw them to the proverbial wolves.

The Norwegian poem sums it up best in my opinion, especially the part about giving scant choice. If you have nothing or in any state of need you have little choice. You either deal with it or go without. If you look at need it is something you have to have, not just want. Sometimes going without means being in a very bad place. Being homeless in winter is not fun at all. Losing one's house because of gambling debt. Forced to work at a grueling low paying job because that's all you can get. Facing withdrawal from a drug is another example..

However, the Anglo-Saxon rune poem seems to indicate that if a need is acted on in time it can be a good thing. Maybe like catching a tumor early enough. Living cheaply, giving up luxury to save money for a rainy day. Realizing you have a problem with drugs, alcohol, gambling, whatever and getting help before the really bad stuff can happen. And in a way it is need that drives the world. To keep the winter theme from the last rune, if you know winter is coming you can prepare for it and thus be able to survive. Necessity being the mother of invention and all.

Maslow's Hierarchy of Need shows precisely the types of need we all have. Think of a pyramid with layers of need. At the bottom is physiological needs; air, water, rest, sleep, nourishment, survivable climate. Next is safety which is shelter, some form of income to meet your needs, self protection, a good mode of transportation. This level of need is about making yourself more comfortable once your basic physical needs are met. After this is the need of love and belonging. Everyone needs to love and to feel loved. To belong to a family that cares about them. After this is esteem, which Maslow broke down into two different levels. The first level is the need to have others respect you. The other level is self respect. After this you have actualization, which is your life's mission. This need never can be satisfied and continuously drives us to go on.

Nauthiz can represent a need on any of these levels. It can also represent what we need to do to overcome these needs. If you have a drug addiction, then get treatment. If you lose your job, then update your resume and start looking for the next job. It is not letting the need rule you but finding ways to get those needs met. It can represent the thing we need rather than what we want. Needs must always take precedence over wants. Thus the rune can cut to the core of necessity.

This rune can be used to help you out of your needs, or to put someone into a state of need. It can also help prepare for times of need.

Isa - Ice

In a world ruled by fire and ice it is only natural to have a rune representing this powerful element. And like other runes this gives rise to contradictory meanings, yet each is appropriate. In each of the first three runes of Hagal's Aett, there have been references to ice and cold. With Hagalaz it represents hail, which is frozen water. The Norwegian poem about Nauthiz talks about being left out in the cold. And Isa is ice itself. In the southern countries heat is the enemy. It can burn your crops and being stuck in the desert will quickly lead to death. But in the north the growing season is short and ice is the great enemy.

Anglo-Saxon Rune Poem:

Ice is over cold, very slippery, it glistens like glass, most like a jewel, a floor made of frost, fair to see.

Norwegian Rune Poem:

[ice] we call the broad bridge; The blind man must be led.

Icelandic Rune Poem:

[ice] = bark of rivers and roof of the wave and destruction of the doomed.

All three rune poems echo similar thoughts about Isa. Ice is hard, slippery and can be treacherous. It is water made solid. Here we see the other creative impulse to the Norse. First is fire and now ice. This idea is especially true in Iceland where you have the natural combination of glaciers and volcanoes. From these two elements everything eventually was created. What does this all mean magically? One's first thoughts tend to go towards blockage, or stoppage. Water no longer flows, but is fixed. Thus this rune can represent an obstacle, or blockage for movement. We have seen with Fehu and Uruz how important movement and circulation can be in regards to wealth and health. Thus Isa can have a negative association of lack of progress and possibly stagnation if blocked for too long. Magically it could be used to put blocks or obstacles in the way of others (or oneself). Or there may be other times where stopping something is worthwhile, like stopping a wound from bleeding. Or stopping diarrhea.

Liquid turning into solid can relate to manifestation of goals, energy and ideas. A person will sink when stepping into a tub of water, but can stand on a tub of ice, thus reaching higher than they could otherwise. Water is fluid without shape. But ice can be sculpted into a variety of shapes, even whole hotels. In this way Isa can represent the solidification of one's desires into reality. Magically speaking this is quite powerful and useful and makes sense when looking at ice as the other half of the great creative impulse.

Thirdly it can represent a bridge, as mentioned in the Norwegian poem. In fact all three poems mention something along these lines. A river that is too wide to swim across, come winter time can be walked across when it freezes. Water, in this case normally an impediment, has become a way to reach one's destination. Granted ice is slippery and one must take care when crossing to make sure the ice is actually solid or to not fall down. It will melt and vanish again in the spring. However ice can also represent a rigidity of ideas or notions that might be unhealthy and keep us from moving forward or making progress in our lives. Water, being a fluid can't be hurt, but ice can shatter. Isa is, in my opinion, a lesson to not be too unbending or like an icicle you will break. Physically it can be tension, worries that have solidified within us as water solidifies into ice. Stress can take its toll on a person and lead to destruction just as surely as if you froze to death camping on a glacier.

During my early days of using runes in my Reiki practice I found that you could substitute runes for the Reiki symbols. Algiz worked in place of the Reiki Power symbol, Isa worked just fine instead of the Distance Symbol. I could, in effect, do Reiki using only runes. It was exhilarating and also verification of various rune meanings. It showed that yes, Isa can act as a bridge and connect two places together. My Reiki teachers noticed that the energy seemed a bit rougher, a little more untamed than normal Reiki energy, but it was proof of concept and this was the first step in developing the system I now call Rún Valdr.

Jera - Year

Anglo-Saxon Rune Poem:

> *The Season is hopeful when heaven's*
> *king allows the fields to blossom forth a*
> *bright abundance for rich and poor.*

Norwegian Rune Poem:

> *[plenty] is a boon to men; I say that*
> *Frothi was generous.*

Icelandic Rune Poem:

> *[plenty] = boon to men*
> *and good summer*
> *and thriving crops.*

Jera is deceptively simple. While it simply means the year, it encompasses several different layers. First think of a harvest cycle. The land rejuvenates through the winter, is planted in the spring, tended during the summer and harvested in the fall. In a way it represents the harvest from good work. Put in the work, and in the fullness of time you will get results. The representations of the year and the work within that year can be thought of in terms of "right timing;" that is, things will happen at the right time, just like the harvest follows the planting. The harvest never comes before the planting, nor does winter come after spring. The proper action must happen in the proper time frame. Jera could be a warning to make sure the proper steps are taken to insure good results, or it could tell you that things are on the proper track. It also may be telling you to slow down and enjoy the process. You can't rush the growing season. I believe this rune is less goal oriented and more process oriented. However, as an indicator of timing you are talking about a longer time frame. Dagaz, the day, can be seen as a much quicker time frame as far as results go. So if Jera comes up in a divination, in terms of results, it could indicate that it will be awhile yet

The shape of Jera is reminiscent of the yin yang symbol in that you can see a duality spinning about a central point. Summer leads to winter which leads to summer, etc. And since the Norse only recognized two seasons, summer and winter you can see this in the rune itself. This is a dynamic rune, but a slower, deeper kind of dynamism. Winter still sees the sun in the sky, even though its power is diminished. Summer still sees the importance of cool water to help life grow under the power of the sun. This is much like how the yin has some yang and the yang has some yin. Sowilo, the sun, is also made up of the same basic shapes, but configured a little differently. It also shows a dynamism as the sun spins above us showering us with warmth and drives the seasons. Ingwaz has the same shapes, but the configuration is closed showing a protective seed, full of the promise of growth, thus is potential movement.

Jera being the fruitful year where one harvests abundance can also indicate abundance and in a negative context could indicate lack of abundance. In either case this abundance, or lack thereof, is the result of our actions. Time is always moving from one season to the next. If you prepare and put in the work, you can take advantage of this cycle. If you waste your time and don't prepare, you will be lacking when the cycle moves along. Much like the story of the ant and the grasshopper.

To some degree that is what all divination is about. From pulling lots to tarot cards, to fire scrying, to looking at astrology, it is all about finding out the right timing of things or determining the cosmic tide so one doesn't waste time trying to move against it.

In a magical working I would use Jera to insure that everything falls into the proper place according to your goal. Thus you can focus on the goal and allow Jera to insure the proper steps are done at the proper time. Especially long term goals.

Eiwaz - World Tree

Anglo-Saxon Rune Poem:

[the yew] is a tree with rough bark, hard
and fast in the earth supported by its
roots, a guardian of flame and a joy upon
an estate.

Norwegian Rune Poem:

[yew] is the greenest of trees in winter; It
is wont to crackle when it burns.

Icelandic Rune Poem:

[yew] = bent bow
and brittle iron
and Giant of the arrow.

For the longest time I saw Eiwaz as a rune of death. However it seems to be more related to initiations and shamanic type of work, especially that of astral projection or even mental journeys one may take to visit those of the otherworlds. There was one Lughnasadh ritual from my Grove that shows this association fairly well. As is the usual custom our Lughnasadh was to honor our tribal father Lugh who is wed to Ana, our local river Goddess. It is my understanding that when a Celtic people moved into a new land they would wed their Sky Father God with the local River Goddess, thus insuring they had access to Her bounty and abundance, a right to live in that land. My Grove did something similar with Lugh and Ana. We take time at Lughnasadh to honor them both. At this particular Lughnasadh, we were planning on having the main rite on Saturday and then on Sunday to have some other workshops including a guided meditation to meet both Lugh and Ana. During the ritual we had a bad omen. When asked what we needed to do to make things right I had a very difficult answer. I found it hard to interpret. I drew extra runes and tried like crazy to make sense of what I got. Eiwaz played a big part. After some time the meaning became clear. Lugh and Ana wanted us to visit Them now. So I did an impromptu guided meditation and everyone met the two Deities. We then got a good omen and resumed the rest of the ritual. Later, the planned guided meditation was canceled. So it seemed that this was known to Lugh and Ana who still wanted the chance to meet us all. The lesson I took from this, aside from the obvious, was that Eiwaz was a rune associated with interaction with the world beyond Midgard, the physical realm we all know so well. The shape of the rune suggests movement back and forth between two places. It is not a one way street as would be the last journey represented by death, but a give and take and travel there and back again.

Indeed some authors talk about initiation associations with this rune, which would fit in with the interaction with the otherworld theme that I favor. Thorsson in particular talks about the toxins in yew trees being able to be turned into hallucinogens. Also, according to Thorsson, yew trees can give of a toxic gas that cane give hallucinations to those who sit under it making trance journey work easier. Thorsson, Aswynn, and Gundarsson all relate this rune to the world tree, Yggdrasil. Since the Yggdrasil connects all the worlds, a natural connection between this rune and travelling the different worlds is made. Seidh and other shamanic like activities then fall under the prevue of this rune.

Freya Aswynn associates this rune with the back and the backbone. In a reading it can indicate back trouble. It can also represent a "strong backbone," the assertiveness to get the job done and the ability to stiffen one's spine in order to overcome obstacles and to face challenges. The Anglo-Saxon poem talks about how strong and well supported the yew tree is. The Norse poem talks about how green this tree is in the winter. Hardly a vision of death, but instead one of life, overcoming the hardship and barrenness of winter. And yet the Icelandic poem seems to suggest that we should still have some flexibility. Yew has long been used for bows and brittle iron, while hard, can shatter if tested. But a yew bow gives life and thrust and deadly energy to an arrow, sending it on its way. The lesson then is to be strong and firm whether in this world or when dealing with the others, but don't be so firm that you become brittle. A bit of flexibility is called for as well.

It should also be noted that the Norse and Icelandic Younger Futhark rune looks like an upside down Algiz. But the rune means "yew," and is fitting to discuss with Eiwaz which also is associated with Yew in the Anglo-Saxon poem.

Peorth, Perthro, Peord - Dice Cup (the letter P)

This rune is a source of problem and contention in my mind. Everyone talks about it meaning dice cup and fate, some talk about it as though it were a womb, or a well and then start talking about orlog and the Norns. R.I. Page lists as the meaning of the name as "the letter P" and lists two or three names. He also comments that the name is hard to pin down. Even the different translation of the Anglo-Saxon rune poem have a wide degree of meanings. It seems like no one can really make up their minds what this rune is all about. And in a really funny train of thought, the various names of the P-rune are very similar to Indo-European words meaning "fart." The Albanian word Pjerdh is very close to Peorth, and Peord is close to Greek Perdo. Were the ancients having a laugh? One can argue that most if not all meanings written in books these days are modern meanings that might or might not have nothing to do with how the ancients saw this rune. It is this problem that makes this rune problematic and hard to nail down in terms of good meaning and use.

This rune does not appear in the Younger Futhark so there are no corresponding Norwegian or Icelandic poems about it. I'll list the Dickins and Osborn & Longland translations for you to compare.

Anglo-Saxon Rune Poem (Dickins):

[the chessmen?] is a source of recreation
and amusement to the great, where
warriors sit blithely together in the
banqueting-hall.

Anglo-Saxon Rune Poem (Osborn & Longland):

A lively Tune means laughter and games
where brave folk sit in the banquet hall,
beer-drinking warriors blithe together.

I've seen other translations as dice cup. Despite this translation weirdness it appears that the rune would have something to do with hanging out with friends having a good time, drinking and socializing. Freyja Aswynn claims that instead of warriors and beer hall the older translation was women and birth hall and thus relates this rune to giving birth. Gundarsson likens it to a well and connect it with Uruz and Laguz. Where Laguz is the water itself, Uruz is the flow of the water and Peorth is the well from which the water springs. One could also talk about how it is the earth that holds the seed, which is just as important as the seed itself in order for that seed to grow. If the soil is lacking in proper nutrients, or has the wrong pH, or lack of water, then the seed will not grow, or grow badly.

It can't be denied that the rune looks like a box or cave, cauldron, or womb even, so it is easy to see why this kind of interpretation is so popular. And also why the Anglo-Saxon poem is so often translated as "dice-cup." Once you say it means dice cup you talk about gambling away your freedom and that leads to the subject of fate, making this a rune of fate and the mysteries of fate, of leaving your life to fortune. You can link this with orlog and/or wyrd in that it can be likened to the soil in which the seed of our life grows. Based upon each of our past experiences we have determined if our "life soil", if you will, is good to nurture the seed and plant of our life.

Orlog and wyrd need to be discussed in greater detail. Both terms seem to deal with fate, but after some research they each have different functions and definitions. They work together to create what we can describe as "fate."

Orlog means "primal law" or "primal layer." It is the buildup of past actions that each person, and humanity as a whole has done. A person is not just the result of their past actions, but the actions before they are born; of their parents and ancestors and even the actions of society at the time of their birth. For instance, a person born in a third world country to poverty is different from someone born into a first world country to a wealthy family. One must look at all the past actions that led to that person being born at that time and place. Orlog can be seen a fixed, because you cannot change the past. What has happened is fixed forever. But orlog is not just the past, it recognizes that this past has momentum, weight and a vector that acts upon the present moment to create the future. All this momentum can be read so we may see where this current of orlog will take us.

Wyrd comes from the Anglo-Saxon and generally translates as "fate." Freya Aswynn says it roughly corresponds to the Eastern concept of "karma," and that it can be personal or relate to whole families. It is not fixed and can be changed, unlike orlog. Swain Wódening describes it as a tree or a great web/cloth upon a loom, which shows the interconnectedness of all things so that every deed affects all other things to some degree. Wyrd is the process of orlog (the past actions that are pushing against the now) moving forward from the present into the future. It is seen as a web, because none of us exist in a vacuum. All of our actions affect each other to various degrees, and all of our actions has the weight of orlog behind us. Thus our individual wyrd may clash with other individuals. Nation or cultural wyrd can also clash.

The question of fate is: Can it be changed? I would say yes. The future is always open to change, but we must wrestle with the weight of the orlog behind us, and deal with competing wyrd of others (and their orlog) to change the course we are on. Relating to the rune, Peorth can be seen as our orlog and wyrd interacting together. It is the path our life is taking and the road we walk.

To differentiate it from Raidho; Raidho is the act of traveling one's path in life, Peorth is the path itself, while Ehwaz would be the vehicle we travel in.

Looking at the rune poem, by itself, it seems more likely to represent a hall or other closed place where people meet in a social setting. The poem basically refers to a party where people are enjoying each other's company. Looking at Peorth in this light would suggest that this rune as more related to the social functions between individuals. Humans are social creatures and like to socialize. Hermits and those who stay apart are distrusted. To be outcast or ostracized was a fierce punishment to bestow on individuals. In ancient times you needed to get help from your neighbors. In our modern times it is easier to get by alone.

Strangely our modern urban society encourages aloneness. By living so close to each other constant contact becomes overwhelming. As a defensive mechanism one pulls away, withdraws, so that even in a crowd, one tries to maintain their own space. This breeds a certain amount of apathy where crowds of people fail to help someone being robbed or raped because "they don't want to get involved." There is a saying that good fences make good neighbors. When the nearest neighbor is a mile away, you learn to make friends and lend a hand. When your neighbors are eight feet away above and below you in an apartment building, you spend time trying to ignore their presence.

The Anglo-Saxon poem reminds us that people are social and take pleasure socializing with each other. Having a friend to talk to makes things easier. Social recreation becomes necessary for a society to function properly. So in a way the poem says that Peorth is a get together of people in peace and well being, or frith. This could be an alliance between two groups, or just a gathering of like-minded people. This can be a rune of fate, of one's path in life, a rune of socialization and common goodwill, or in negative light can be a rune of the outcast and one out of balance with one's path. Thus it could be used in attempts to change your orlog. It could also just as easily be used when trying to fit in, or in finding your place.

One can even tie in the older idea, expressed by the poem, of the importance of socialization with the more modern ideas of orlog and wyrd. We live in a sea of orlog and wyrd and by working together, in proper social balance, we can achieve a greater future. Understanding the orlog of someone, where they are coming from, can help to find common ground to negotiate a path together. Ignoring this can lead to conflict and a clash of efforts which helps no one.

Which interpretation is best? Meditate on this rune and find your own path. I would say looking at the social angle, you could us this rune for magical work related to interacting with others in a social setting. Perhaps overcoming shyness, or stage fright if you have to speak in pubic. Or in gathering common consensus on an issue affecting the community as a whole.

Algiz - Elk

The Younger Futhark has this same rune, but it is called Madr, or Man, and thus is more in line with the Elder Futhark rune Mannaz. This confuses things as the same rune have two different sounds associated with them and two different names. Based on the shape the Younger Futhark rune should be discussed with Algiz, but based on sound and name/meaning it should be discussed with Mannaz. This rune also does not have a comparison in the Younger Futhark so there are no accompanying Norwegian or Icelandic poems.

Some authors, Jane Sibley and Edred Thorson, compare this rune to the Younger Futhark rune Yr. Yr looks like an upside down Algiz. Algiz represents the final Z sound in words, which later became a final R sound represented by Yr. But to further complicate things, "z" in Old Norse represented middle voice congugaton/declension. Some words went to an "r" while others to an "s" where the "z" originally was placed. The R sound was rather like "rzh" sound (Jane Sibley, *Some Notes On Rune Traditional Magic, and Runic Divination*, folder, p. 63). Edred Thorsson in Futhark, A Handbook of Rune Magic (SamuelWeiser, 1984, p.48) mentions that the rune was the final grammatical z, which later became the final r in Old Norse. He also says on the next page that the rune is associated with the Gothic word alhs (meaning sanctuary) has been associated with this rune, thus bringing into consideration a divine element.

However, as mentioned with Eiwaz, Yr and the linked Norwegian and Icelandic poems all have a meaning of "yew." Thus the meanings are not compatible and I find that Yr belongs with the Anglo-Saxon yew rune poem.

Anglo-Saxon Rune Poem:

> *Eel-grass grows most often in fen, waxes*
> *in water, grimly wounds, burning with*
> *stripes of blood the one who tries to get a grip on it.*

Looking at the poem it seems to present a definite defensive concept. Not a hit-first kind of defense like we saw with Thurisaz, nor the distraction style protection with Hagalaz. Algiz is more passive, yet just as effective. It presents a difficulty whereby interaction with it will cause harm. But unlike Thurisaz, which seeks out targets, Algiz allows the other person to make the mistake of touching it first, like the effects of a cactus. The poem describes in some detail a type of grass that is very sharp that will cut those who carelessly grabs it. Similar to something being so obvious of a threat that everyone leaves it alone without coming near it, so this rune sits there passively defending the object/person it is sworn to protect.

I have noticed in my own experiments that there is a divine nature to this rune. I see it as the descent of divine energy into the everyday world, which echoes Jane Sibley's idea of Thurisaz. I found that I was able to use runes in place of various Reiki symbols and still get the Reiki system to work. Algiz proved to be quite effective as the Power Symbol from Reiki. It was this experimentation with Algiz than really validated the idea that not only was this rune about protection but of the idea of divine energy flowing downwards to the physical world. This implied a divine interaction with the world as well as with the people living in this world.

In terms of protection and the divine you could say that by filling something with divine energy it would drive away negative influences which cannot stand to be near such holy energy. Thus instead of being merely a physically harmful thing to grasp, it refers to being spiritually harmful to negative beings.

Sowilo - Sun

Anglo-Saxon Rune Poem:

> *The Sun to seafarers always means hope,*
> *when they ferry across the fishes' bath till*
> *the horse of the sea brings them to harbor.*

Norwegian Rune Poem:

> *[sun] is the light of the world; I bow to*
> *the divine decree.*

Icelandic Rune Poem:

> *[sun] = shield of the clouds*
> *and shining ray*
> *and destroyer of ice.*

This rune represents the sun. For the ancient northern Europeans the sun was of vital importance. With the short growing season the sun literally meant the difference between life and death. All the rune poems seem to see the sun as a good thing. It can help one navigate, it destroys ice and it is the divine showering the world with power and life. It is interesting that the ancient Germanic people saw the sun as female and the moon as female. This is opposite of the viewpoints of the southern Europeans. I like to think this is the case because in the far north the sun was nurturing and dear. After all the growing season was short as was the summer. The sun was essential to life in the north. In the south the sun could burn crops and bring drought while in the north it brought only life and well-being. It is not surprising that sun cults were popular and that the sun was seen as a source of divine energy and life.

The Anglo-Saxon poem has good examples of kennings. Fishes' bath is the ocean and the horse of the sea is a ship. The poem talks about the sun as a navigation tool. Not only does it provide light, but it allowed early sailors to find their way. For a sea-faring people navigation was vital. The sun allowed them to chart courses on the open sea, freeing them to make longer voyages. It also led to the discovery of Iceland, Greenland, and the Americas, allowing the Norse to visit these places before any other Europeans. The sun can be seen as a guiding influence, leading us on our path. Magically, you could use this aspect of the rune in situations where you feel lost and need some help in navigating your life.

The Norwegian poem focus on the holy aspect of the sun. In my opinion, this is the key poem describing this rune. I see it as the outpouring of divine energy. In this sense it could be used for purification as well as for hallowing. In addition to this, it can be used for success in endeavors by bringing divine might to bear on the situation.

The Icelandic poem talks about the pragmatic virtues of the sun to melt ice and to protect from the cold. This poem shows the importance of the sun to the Northern peoples. It literally was life, and without it they would die. The growing season was short, and they needed to make the most of the summer and the heat of the sun.

This is a good general rune to use in almost any working. Looking at the runes by themselves, this rune is probably the most holy. Use it in a working if you need an infusion of divine energy.

Tyr's Aett

Tiwaz - The God Tyr

Anglo-Saxon Rune Poem:

[Tiw?] is a (guiding) star; well does it keeps faith with princes; it is ever on its course over the mists of night and never fails.

Norwegian Rune Poem:

[Tyr] is a one handed god; Often has the smith to blow.

Icelandic Rune Poem:

[Tyr] = god with one hand and leavings of the wolf and prince of temples.

Tiwaz represents the god Tyr (Tiw) and we can glean quite a few things from the poems. It is interesting to note that in the Anglo-Saxon rune poem that it pretty much focuses on star imagery. I would say that the star in question represents the North Star. This star, unwavering, and seemingly, unmoving fits the bill of keeping faith and never failing. As we have seen with the previous rune, while the Sun is vital to navigation during the day, the North Star is the counterpart during the night. This poem speaks of steadfastness and dependability. The unwavering nature of the star mirrors the unwavering nature of Tyr as He sacrificed His hand. It is because of this that Tyr is associated with legal and lawfulness and has come to represent the letter of the law. Because Tyr is a war god, it is tempting to think that the star mentioned is the planet Mars. Mars, however, is not typically seen as a guiding star like the North Star is.

He is seen as a god of justice and "doing what is necessary" as well as a god of war. This is based on the story of the binding of the great wolf Fenris. Growing great in size, the gods were alarmed and sought a means to bind him. The gods used several different chains, making a game to see of Fenris could break them, which he could. Finally the gods got a thin ribbon made up of impossible things; fishes breath, the sound of cat's footfall, a woman's beard, etc (which is why these things no longer exist in the mundane world). Being suspicious of the very thin rope, Fenris would only agree to be bound if someone would place their hand in his mouth. If he could not break free, he would then eat the hand. None of the gods wanted to step forward, but at last Tyr did and placed His hand in the mouth of Fenris. He knew that He would lose his hand, but did it anyway. Upon testing the rope Fenris found he could not break it and promptly bit off Tyr's hand. At last the great wolf was bound, safe until the time of Ragnarok.

Both the Norwegian and Icelandic poems mention that Tyr has only one hand and thus fall in line with the legends. If you are looking for a rune to make contact with the God Tyr than this is the one for you. I would suggest meditating upon the rune combined with prayers to Tyr. The obvious reference to the story of Tyr and Fenris show the steadfast nature of Tyr and the willingness to do what is necessary even at personal sacrifice.

Edred Thorsson and Diana Paxson speak of associations with the irminsul, which as far as my research suggests, was a pillar erected in the open air and used as a worship focus among the Germanic people. There are quite a few historical references to these pillars including some that had statues of gods on top of them. The shape of Tiwaz and the reference of the Icelandic poem about Tyr being the prince of temples would further suggest a connection with the concept of the irminsul. If one sees the irminsul as holding up society and religion then the Anglo-Saxon reference of the North Star makes some sense as this star upheld the lawfulness of the sky and brought direction and guidance to ancient sailors. The shape of the rune suggests a spear, and or the shape of the Irminsul pillar.

According to Jane Sibley, a lot of the use of Tiwaz was in both warrior spells and mortuary charms. For warriors the rune was used to inspire courage. Sibley also says that Tyr runes were carved on the soles of shoes of the dead to give them courage to make the journey to Hel. Common forms were triple Tiwaz runes.

This rune has come to represent law and rightness of action. It can be used if one is facing legal issues, however you should be very sure you are legally in the right, or it could backfire on you.

Historically it has been used for success and many weapons were engraved with this rune for magical aid in battle as Tyr was said to have control over victory in battle. I find that it is also a very masculine rune and the shape is rather phallic in nature. So if there is a need for masculine energy in your workings, then this is a good rune to use. Looking at the steadfast nature I would imagine it could be used when trying to develop good behaviors such as setting up a consistent exercise routine.

Berkano - Birch

Anglo-Saxon Rune Poem:

> *The Poplar is fruit-less, even so puts*
>
> *forth shoots without seeding,*
>
> *has shining*
>
> *branches high in an ornamented helmet,*
>
> *laden with leaves, in touch with the sky.*

Norwegian Rune Poem:

> *[birch] has the greenest leaves of any*
>
> *shrub; Loki was fortunate in his deceit.*

Icelandic Rune Poem:

> *[birch] = leafy twig*
>
> *and little tree*
>
> *and fresh young shrub.*

Whereas Tiwaz is a very masculine rune, I find Berkano to be rather feminine. All the poems talk about trees, Birch for Norwegian and Icelandic and Poplar for Anglo-Saxon. Diane Paxson comments in *Taking Up The Runes* that this is rather odd and that Osborn and Longland are alone with ascribing the poplar tree for this rune. The Anglo-Saxon name Beorc is the word for Birch, but the description in the poem itself is more appropriate for the black poplar with the reference of being fruit-less and putting forth shoots without seeding. However it does mention shining branches which would be more appropriate to the white bark of the birch. I'm content to see this as a birch tree.

Both the Norwegian and Icelandic poems mention birch. Despite the discrepancies between the poems they all describe a tree. The Anglo-Saxon poem seems to be describing something holy and brimming with life, in that it can propagate without seeds. The birch is used in Norse purification usually after visiting a sauna. In this case we can see the birch, and this rune as representing purification and beginning new things.

One can look at this rune and see a pregnant woman in a profile with the rune showing breasts and belly. This further reinforces the idea of new things (babies representing new life, new members of the community). It also points to my feeling that this is a feminine rune. A lot of authors talk about a birch goddess or a goddess in general in association with this rune. Thorsson associates this rune with the Earth Mother. Gundarsson specifically with Nerthus. Diana Paxson associates Berkano with Frigga, as the most motherly goddess.

Paxson mentions that this rune could be considered a healing rune based upon the medicinal properties of birch leaves and birch oil. While the virtuous properties of birch cannot be denied I'm not seeing this in direct connection with the rune poems. Not that this invalidates the healing notion at all, but I'm always one to stick to the original source material as much as possible. Paxson also mentions that it was a Scandinavian tradition for lads to carry birch twigs on May Day in a procession to celebrate the return of vegetation. Freyja Aswynn mentions that in Holland the May Day rites included whipping women with birch branches for fertility. This echoes the Norse idea of switching oneself with a birch branch for purification after a sauna. Elizabethan writer Phillip Stubbes in his 1583 work *Anatomie of Abuses*, writes with great shock and disapproval of a common practice of folks going out in to woods around May Day to have sex during the evening and return in the morning with birch branches for home decorations and a birch tree for the May Pole. Of course he described the activities as satanic, but it further associates the birch with fertility. He was shocked not only by the groups of people heading out into the woods to "defile" maidens, but that they would dance around a May Pole like heathens worshipping some idol.

The Icelandic poem could seem to suggest a renewal in association with this rune with the "and fresh young shrub" line. The Norwegian poem mentions that "Loki was fortunate in his deceit." This is kind of vague as Loki was fortunate in quite a few deceits. With the other runes seemingly talking about life and renewal, one could associate this rune with Idunna, the keeper of the golden apples that give the Gods immortality and youth, as well as the story of Loki giving Her to the Giants and then rescuing Her from them. Or, since the poems mention a shrub, it could be referring to mistletoe, the item Loki used in the killing of Baldr.

Personally, I find Berkano can be used for fertility, renewal, beginning new endeavors, purification, feminine issues, childbirth or things pertaining to motherhood. It is a very life affirming rune.

Ehwaz - Horse

Anglo-Saxon Rune Poem:

[the horse] is a joy to princes in the
presence of warriors, a steed in the pride
of its hoofs, when rich men on horseback
bandy words about it; and it is ever a
source of comfort to the restless.

The focus of this rune poem is horses. While Raidho can be interpreted as the act of moving or riding/traveling, it is Ehwaz that provides the vehicle for this journey. Horses, in the ancient world, were the automobiles of their time. Much as in the world today, people took pride in their vehicles and they were often seen as status symbols. Owning a horse required a certain amount of upkeep and thus wealth. Feeding, grooming, not to mention training were required. In addition one had to maintain a saddle and horse shoes and other equipment. Today owning a car requires buying fuel, insurance, driving licenses, and the various mechanical upkeep needed to keep it running. Even today cars are objects of status and there are many events devoted exclusively to displaying one's vehicle. However, much like owning a car today, having a horse meant mobility and freedom as is stated in the last line of the poem, as it made longer journeys possible. Likewise

When we discuss vehicles, we can extend this to our bodies as well to any other vehicle whether truck or space shuttle. Traveling with a horse was such an important thing in the past. It became a partnership. Such a partnership can be seen in contemporary times with the 2004 film Hidalgo, which tells the story of a man who competes in long distance horse races. The relationship he had with his horse was almost as strong as or stronger than any he had with other humans. As a note on the importance of this relationship, the movie was named after the horse. On the long road you had to trust your horse and to care for it in return. It is this sense of partnership that is the reason many authors see this rune related to marriage and a rune of relationships. Any relationship depends on both people to maintain it. Together one can do more than by oneself and that is the real lesson if this rune. If one were to go further, Ehwaz might call for the care of one's own body as well since the body is the vehicle for the soul. Bodies, like horses and relationships need work to stay healthy and functional.

This whole rune is devoted to vehicles and to the body itself. It celebrates these bodies that we travel the world in, and the relationship we have with them, whether one thinks about the love of one's car (or horse) or one's own body image. For a while, early on in the development of Rún Valdr, I considered using certain runes to help target the working towards specific goals. Ehwaz was to be used if you wanted to target the body in your working. Mannaz was for the conscious mind and Laguz was for the subconscious mind. The particular symbol would be used early in the programming of the working as a focus for the intent of the working. I never really used this technique much however, as intention worked just as well, but it is still a valid idea in my opinion.

Ehwaz can be used when dealing with issues of the body in general or vehicles for that matter. It is also useful for workings with relationships or partnerships. If you have to negotiate with people this rune, along with Gebo could be used to some advantage.

Mannaz - Mankind

Anglo-Saxon Rune Poem:

Consciousness (individual)
Collective consciousness
Community/society

> *A Man in his gladness is dear to his*
> *kinsman; Yet each must fail the friend he*
> *loves for the Lord in his judgment will*
> *allot that unfortunate flesh to the earth.*

Norwegian Rune Poem:

> *[man] is an augmentation of the dust;*
> *Great is the claw of the hawk.*

Icelandic Rune Poem:

> *[man] = delight of man*
> *and augmentation of the earth*
> *and adorner of ships.*

It should be noted that in the Younger Futhark the M rune is the same shape as Algiz. Thus the line in the Norwegian poem about "Great is the claw of the hawk," seems to indicate the shape of the more modern version of the rune. Regardless of shape, I have to go with the meaning, which is Man, or more appropriately, Mankind. All three poems seem kind of gloomy. No matter how great humans are, they will eventually die. The lines "allot that unfortunate flesh to the earth," "is an augmentation of the dust," and "augmentation of the earth," all suggest burial as one's ultimate fate. By this token we can see that this rune is about humankind specifically rather than the gods or spirits of nature or interactions between the different groups. Modern authors talk about how this is a thought, or hugr (Old Norse), rune indicating the conscious mind and memory, thus it can be beneficial to use when studying. Our consciousness sets us apart from the animals who lack the same level of self awareness and intelligence that humans have. With our minds we have conceived and built huge cities, and amazing invention that do everything from cooking our food to taking us to the moon. Our modern society and technology is a testament to our minds and capabilities.

Beyond the ideas of the conscious mind is human community. The Anglo-Saxon poem says, "A Man in his gladness is dear to his kinsman." And the Icelandic poem says, "Man - delight of man." Thus we see that humans are social beings. This is backed up by several verses from the Havamal. The first stanza says,

"Young and alone on a long road,
Once I lost my way:
Rich I felt when I found another;
Man rejoices in man,"

This stanza echoes the rune poems. It reminds us that we need to rely on our fellow humans and thus teaches the importance of proper social behavior. Outlaws were cast out and could not seek shelter from people. This was one of the worst punishment an ancient Norse could experience, not only because they were forbidden aid from others, but they were outside the bounds of normal society. Killing an outlaw had no legal penalties. In an age where one depended on others to survive, this was a stiff penalty. Another stanza from the Havamal emphasizes this aspect.

"Cattle die, kindred die
Every man is mortal:
But the good name never dies
Of one who has done well"

 This is the promise of immortality, one's good name. It doesn't promise physical immortality, but a great man is remembered by descendants and those that come after. With paganism's focus on the material world this rune teaches us that by walking a good path not only will you have good friends, but you will be remembered. This rune celebrates humans and human society with all the benefits and woe that this can bring.

Magically speaking this rune can be used for help with memory, or when dealing with the conscious mind. Also when dealing with issues of humanity or community or one's place in society. In terms of consciousness and humankind, this rune may be able to tap into the collective consciousness of mankind, something like the Akashic records. Wikipeia defines Akashic records as "In theosophy and anthroposohy, the Akashic records (a term coined in the late 19th century fram akasha or ākāśa, the Sanskrit word for "sky", "space", "luminous", or "aether") are a compendium of thoughts, events, and emotions believed by Theosophists to be encoded in a non-physical plane of existence known as the astral plane."

I'm sure within the collective consciousness there are many treasures to be found. If such a record exists, then I feel the rune of the mind and human consciousness can help one access this. Also, the World Tree, Yggdrasil, in my opinion, acts as the Akashic record keeper for the Northern cultures. Since it touches all the worlds, I believe that it acts a repository of knowledge for the Nine Realms.

Combined with Peorth, Mannaz could be good to deal with social anxieties, or to help insure a productive meeting, or social gathering. I would also use it to help with memory,

Laguz - Water

Anglo-Saxon Rune Poem:

> *Water to landsmen seems overly long if*
> *they must go on the galloping ship, and*
> *the sea-waves scare them excessively,*
> *and the horse of the sea heeds not it's*
> *bridle.*

Norwegian Rune Poem:

> *A [waterfall] is a river which falls from a*
> *mount-side; But ornaments are of gold.*

Icelandic Rune Poem:

> *[water] = eddying stream*
> *and broad geyser*
> *and land of the fish*

Water is the lifeblood of this planet. We can exist only a few days without it. Yet at the same time it can drown us and flood our lands and homes bringing great destruction and death. Ships can be lost at sea or sunk on rocks not seen below the surface not to mention icebergs. For the early Norse, who traveled extensively on ships, water was a blessing and a curse. It gave them access for trading and raiding, yet it also could mean drowning far from home. The rune poems all touch upon some aspect of water. The Anglo-Saxon talks about how the sea can be a fearful thing. The Norwegian poem talks about a waterfall, and perhaps a reference to finding gold, which can be found in streams. Or it could be saying that while waterfalls are beautiful, only gold can be worn. Or that both water and gold are precious. The Icelandic poem takes a broader look, looking at streams, geysers and talks about fish, a great source of food. To this day Iceland is very reliant upon the fishing industry to bolster its economy.

We can look at water in two ways when dealing with divination. On one hand water is necessary for life, but on the other too much can bring death and destruction, as we see with tsunamis and other floods. We can say that on a positive note this rune brings that which is necessary. In a more negative aspect it will bring disaster, however this disaster will be too much of a good thing rather than random destructive forces. In a relationship question this could indicate having what is necessary for a good relationship, or it could represent an obsessive affection that will only spell ruin. Or perhaps needing a relationship to such an extent that you ruin it by over thinking and doing too much and then being obsessive about it. Being in a relationship for the sake of being in a relationship rather than naturally forming a bond with someone.

Water also contains treasures, not always obvious. How many fishermen see their prize before it bites the line or is caught in a net? How many times can you see the gold in a streambed before it ends up in the pan? The sea and lakes have a lot hidden beneath when you only look at the surface. Looking at water this way makes me think of our own subconscious minds. There is a lot under the surface of our consciousness that truly define who we are much more than the face we show the world. Because if this, I tend to see Laguz as associated with the subconscious mind while Mannaz deals with the conscious. Thus Laguz can represent that which is hidden, like the fish hidden from the surface or the subconscious mind hidden from the conscious. Looking at this rune my first thought is always that it means something hidden away. Indeed looking at the above statement about too much of a good thing, many mental problems can be seen as an unhealthy obsession with something, where the subconscious is out of balance. So this rune could help with subconscious mental health. However water brings life and our planet would be dead without it. Magically it can be used in cases where water is important or for things that are hidden, or as mentioned for insuring that you have what you need to survive or succeed.

Ingwaz - The God Freyr

Anglo-Saxon Rune Poem:

Ing at first was seen by folk among the
East Danes, till afterwards he went over
the waves, followed his wagon. Thus the
Heardings named this hero.

According to the book Our Troth: volume 1, History and Lore "Norse references to him [Freyr] as Yngvi-Freyr or Ingunar-Freyr have led to the conclusion that he is the same god as the Anglo-Saxon Ing and the Gothic Engus." (Our Troth, Gundarsson, page 251). In fact most modern authors agree that this rune represents the god Freyr. It then behooves us to look at the aspects of Freyr to gain inside into the nature of this rune.

The Troth book mentions several aspects of Freyr, as a God of fighting, but only if necessary to keep the peace, also defending those in battle, and mentions that "[Freyr] loves peace so much that he is willing to fight to keep it" (Our Troth, page 254-255), a Peace God who spreads frith and a keeper of peace, (Our Troth, page 255), a God of the Howe, or burial mound and also as an ancestor God. Both Odin and Freyr have spawned human king dynasties (Our Troth, page 256), and a God of the fruitfulness of the land as seen in Freyr's marriage to the Giantess Gerðr (Our Troth, page 258).

It is this last aspect that bears looking into further. The poem mentions traveling in a wagon, this was a common practice among worshippers of Nerthus who would parade her statue in a wagon about the countryside to bring prosperity. One can conclude that such a practice was a common Vanir practice as both Freyr and Nerthus are counted among the Vanir, even though Nerthus is Germanic in origin rather than Norse. It also establishes that Freyr was important for bringing prosperity to the land. The poem also says that He moves East to West, much like the life-giving sun, which would suggest a solar association with Freyr. As we saw when looking at the rune Sowilo, the sun was hugely important to the Northern people.

Regarding the story of how Freyr woos the Giantess Gerðr we can interpret it as the power of taming the wild to make it fruitful. In the story, Freyr sits on Odin's chair, Hlidskjalf, and sees from afar the giant maid, Gerðr, and falls in love with her. Freyr then pines for her as he realizes that such a union would not be approved. This shows his keeping with frith as he only involves himself and chooses not to upset the frith between the Aesir/Vanir and the Jotuns. His pining is noticed by others and he is urged to do something about it. Freyr ends up sending his servant, Skirnir (Radiance), to woo Gerðr for him. As is mentioned in Our Troth (page 258) the story outlines the customary formula of courtship, first gifts (Freyr's sword and horse), then threat of ritual abduction. Here Gerðr mentions the might of her own kin so that abduction would not avail him. Then Skirnir threatens to curse her and thus gives a choice; either Gerðr accepts Freyr, becoming fruitful and renewing the earth, or she can reject him and become barren and ugly like other monstrous Giant women. The lesson here is that Freyr can bring abundance and fruitfulness to the earth (Gerðr) and without his presence the land would become barren. Also significant is that it shows the gods' ability to tame the wildness (metaphor for agriculture) in order for it to be more useful and thus safer for humans and the gods. Or at least Freyr can do this, especially if He has solar associations.

Many modern authors liken this rune to a seed, some to a scrotum sack, which shows that the rune is full of potential. It is not a rune of action and looking at the imagery you can see that even though it is made up of energetic chevrons, they are locked together into a still form. This perfectly fits the idea of a seed, where a tiny object has the potential to grow into a mighty tree, or a fruit bearing bush that produces much fruit and further seeds. It is the miracle of agriculture. From one seed many, many, more can be produced. This rune is about potential, that spark of life that is ready to burst forth. Ingwaz teaches us that we can find the seed within us that if nurtured, can grow.

This can be extrapolated to pure human sexuality and fertility to agriculture prosperity to creativity where, as Odin said in stanza 141 of the Havamal, "one word lead to another word and one deed led to another deed." The Anglo-Saxon version of this rune look similar to a DNA strand, thus showing the potential within each of us and of humans in general.

This rune shows great potential, but like any potential it must be realized. It is the ground work necessary to have success. It is the planting before the harvesting, the planning before a successful business venture (or even battle), the designing of a painting before brush is put to canvas, the planning of a child before conception is started. Magically speaking, Ingwaz can be combined with Jera, to make sure the outcome not only fits into the proper cycle or timing, but that the proper gestation period is adhered to so that you don't try to push results too quickly. The Vanir custom of parading idols of Freyr and Nerthus is to bring fruitfulness to the land before anything is planted. The work to realize that potential still has to be done. Without the prep work, or the potential, nothing will result no matter how hard one works. Barrenness will yield no fruit. If you have no clue how to proceed you will fail. Ingwaz can be used to insure that there is enough raw potential to gain the results you want.

Dagaz - Day

Anglo-Saxon Rune Poem:

> *Day, God's message, is dear to men; The*
> *great Lord's light means gladness and*
> *hope to rich and poor, a profit to all.*

In terms of divination this rune has always been one of the hardest for me to interpret. It seems to represent such abstract concepts that trying to get a practical interpretation is difficult at best. I've always hated when this rune comes up in a reading. A day is not just when the sun is in the sky, but includes the night portion as well. Many ancient societies started a day with dusk. The rune poem would seem to indicate that this rune can bring gladness, hope and profit. But we must ask in what way? However the phrase, "The great Lord's light means…" would seem to indicate that we are talking about when the sun is in the sky. Was the night so terrifying that seeing the sun brought such hope? I can see it being profitable to all because in the day time one can do work. It is interesting to see a shift from a day being made up of the dark and light parts to only talking about the light part. One can tell from the language that this particular poem has strong Christian overtones. Thus any older associations may have been lost. It could just mean that with a new day we have another opportunity to prosper and do well. In this case it is the hope of a new day that is important. With another day comes another chance to make a difference. Thus in a divination it could mean a second chance, or a brief renewal.

Even if we just look at the part of a day when the sun is out, what is a day? It is a specified unit of time similar to Jera. But where Jera represented a whole year, Dagaz only reflects a day and points to a short time frame in terms of timing of events. This timing could be used for magical works as well, to delineate fast results, or to set limits on how long the magic will last. Looking at the day cycle of day and night where it is not just when the sun is out that counts, but the dark time too brings to mind liminal space. You have at least twice a day a time when the light and dark mingle together where you have a time that is neither fully dark, nor fully light. This kind of liminal space is always important magically. Since it is in between things it is not one or the other. Things are in flux making magic easier to do. So this rune, in my mind, can indicate those liminal spaces where the magic lives, or it could indicate a phase shift between two things. A shift in tide, day to dark, dark to day. By the same token it could also signify two forces, normally opposed, working together. Day and night each are very different from the other, but you need both for a day to function properly. Thus harmony is achieved from unlikely partners. Looking at this rune further I can see new meanings than just short term timing and liminal space. Hope and the working together of different forces adds to the repertoire of meanings.

Difficulty with divination aside, Dagaz can be useful rom a magical point of view. It would be great to get arguing factions to work together, to instill hope and a renewal of purpose. Speaking of hope, perhaps it could be used in an anti-depression capacity. It can also be used to insure a quick manifestation of results during a shorter time frame. It could also be used to help create liminal space, perhaps for ritual or magical work where such things are important. Especially combined with Othala which could be used to create a safe space to do ritual.

Othala - Home

Anglo-Saxon Rune Poem:

*[an estate] is very dear to every man, if he
can enjoy there in his house whatever is
right and proper in constant prosperity.*

This is the rune of the home. It is what is known and safe. Not only that, but the rune poem hints at inheritance with the line about "constant prosperity." A farmer usually intends to leave the holdings to his or her family. To the ancient Norse, few things were more important than family and holding your own land.

There are two concepts that are, in my mind, linked with this rune. The idea of innangard, meaning "within the enclosure" (Old Norse innangarðr) and utangard, meaning "beyond the enclosure" (Old Norse útangarðr). Innangard is that which is known. It is normal society, the home, the village, the safety of home. You can see this in the fences that surrounded farms. Not only was this to allow livestock in, but kept trolls and other hostile things out. The law provided a social innangard, by providing psychological and societal enclosure for safe human behavior. Utangard is that which is unknown and scary. It is alien threats that one is unaccustomed to dealing with outside of safe human society. The punishment for severe crimes was to outlaw the criminal. He or she acted in an utangard fashion and thus was stripped of social protection. Terms used for becoming an outlaw included "going into the forest," which sounds similar to the Norwegian Fehu poem describing "The wolf lives in the forest."

The focus of Othala must be centered on the home and everything that this concept encompasses. One's property, family, ancestors as well as descendants fall within the scope of Othala. While Fehu is mobile wealth, jobs, a career, and Jera can be seen as raw resources, Othala is wealth that is tied to the land and one's family/clan. It is the hearth fire, so important to any hall or home. It is the toil done to make a house a home and the upkeep required to keep it that way. Looking at the ancient Norse sagas one sees over and over that true wealth lay in ownership of land. When the early settlers came to Iceland, they would frequently claim large portions of land. The landowners could then use this land as payment to vassals or given to family members. This is the meaning of the rune poem referring to "right and proper in constant prosperity." Not just as something you leave to your descendants, but as a means of generating wealth. Prosperity was earned from the land and could be given away to spread wealth around. Since one's wealth was measured in how much they could give, the greatest gift was property. It is a gift that keeps on giving.

Getting back to the idea of the innangard/utangard, Othala is a rune that could be used in magic to create a safe space, much as a magic circle is used. It can create a safe place and keep out the unknown and dangerous. Whether this is used in an informal manner or part of a serious and complicated ceremonial setting, this rune can do the job. Run Valdr use of Othala, besides creating a safe space would be to help one get rooted in your core values, those things passed down from generation to generation. It can help to create a safe space within, a sanctuary when times are hard and one is besieged by the unknown. Everyone needs some breathing room and this rune can help create that. When the world is too much and situations overwhelm you, seek solace and comfort in Othala. Similarly it can be used in property claiming rites, used to contact one's ancestors, or to help access ancestral knowledge.

It would also be useful if you want to do work with your ancestors

Stem and Chevron interpretations

Here is a fascinating way of looking at and interpreting the runes to gain further insight into their qualities.

Paul Tuitéan in his book *The Roots of Midgard* talks about the idea that all runes can be broken down into two basic shapes. There are the stem and chevron. Both of these two shapes have different properties. These shapes can be seesn as and , Isa and Kenaz respectively. Chevrons can be any diagonal line, so half chevrons are valid. Thus stems are represented as ice and the chevrons are seen as fire. This echoes the Norse creation story where everything was ultimately created from the combination of primal fire and ice. As runes, Isa can be seen as primal ice while Kenaz fits the role of primal fire. Essentially all runes are made up of various proportions of fire and ice. You can look at each rune and analyze the different compositions of fire and ice that appear within each rune.

Ice associations would be stillness and physicality while fire associations would be activity and non physical energy. Look at Kenaz, Jera, Sowilo, Ingwaz, Othala, and Gebo, all are made exclusively of chevrons, yet their individual characteristics are quite different. Kenaz is, as mentioned primal fire, and gives the basic characteristics of what fire means. Jera, while made up entirely of fire, suggests a balancing action, always moving, like the year itself. It does resemble a yin yang symbol, as I have already mentioned. Sowilo is also moving and can be seen as the constant outpouring of light we get from the sun. While Ingwaz is turned inward into a still form of a seed. Othala's structure already creates a space within it, and unlike Ingwaz, extends outwards, perhaps one towards the ancestors and one towards the descendants. Gebo, while made of fire, seems locked into form. Perhaps this is the old pattern of hospitality. A gift for a gift which creates the fire of community. It is the act of giving that is important.

Isa itself is very solid and still, yet forms the basis of most of the runes. The rest of the runes contain ice, perhaps as a functionality of manifestation. Yet look at Nauthiz and Lagu, both contain one fire and one ice. Both have very different properties. In Nauthiz, the chevron looks stuck or hampered, while with Laguz it looks like it is covering something. You can look at all the runes by how much fire and ice they have and how the shape is put together to gain deeper insights into each rune. It makes for an interesting exercise.

It is worthwhile to meditate and study the runes so that their meanings and ways to work with them become integrated into your consciousness. They are complex and knowing which layer to use over another is key to the effective use of the runes.

If you are new to runes I would recommend doing daily divinations to get used to learning the meanings. Or even pick a rune for the day and let the rune be in the back of your mind as you go through out your day. Try to look for the rune in the world around you. Think about its meanings and how they relate to you.

However, don't let a lack of knowledge keep you from pursuing Rún Valdr. I have heard from others that they do not want to learn Rún Valdr yet because they feel that they need to learn the runes first. Nothing could be further from the truth. This book, and the quick Rún Valdr guides provides a good overview to the meanings of each rune. Rún Valdr provides so many great benefits, please don't let a lack of knowledge of runes stop you. The tools provided by Rún Valdr are too great to be put aside by fear or uncertainty.

Chapter Three
Rún Valdr Symbols

The non-rune symbols are all new and can be considered "channeled" material (UPG) as they were gained from trance journey work. Looking at the symbols one thing that can be noticed (besides they tend to look like crop circles) is that one can look at the image and derive an idea of what they do. The basic guidelines are that the circles are reservoirs of energy and the lines are direction of force. So Shai Nal would be energy coming down and being concentrated. Shambul is energy coming out of a storage area to be used. Grija appears to be an image of a boiling cauldron where the lines are the steam coming up as one burns away impurities. Reloxon obviously connects two points.

A note on pronunciation of the symbol names. Any J in a word is pronounced, in the Scandinavian fashion, as a Y sound, unless specifically stated otherwise. Thus Grija is pronounced Gree-Yah. The letter G is always a hard G sound.

Some symbols have specific colors associated with them. Others don't. As a default all runes and symbols should be seen as gold or red unless a specific color is listed for that symbol. When I first started Rún Valdr I just used the color red, since it was a traditional color for the runes. However at some point I was told, by Odin, to use gold for Shai Nal and ended up using gold as the default color for everything. Gold was a color closely associated with the Gods and also Asgard where They lived and some descriptions have the very stones that make up the street being of gold as well as most of the buildings, etc. In the poem Voluspa from the Poetic Edda, stanza's 7 & 8 give reference to gold and the Gods.

On Itha Plain met the mighty gods;

Shrines and temples they timbered high,

They founded forges to fashion gold,

Tongs they did shape and tools they made;

Played at draughts in the garth: right glad they were,

Nor aught lacked they of lustrous gold –

Till maidens three from the Thurses came,

Awful in might, from etin-home.

Freyja in particular is associated with gold as well. Not only is her necklace gold, but She herself cries tears of gold.

There has been some debate regarding the use of color and its importance in Rún Valdr. I feel that color does make a difference, but have not experimented enough to fully say how. I was told by Odin that one should not use the color black with Shai Nal because it would strip away your emotions. Meaning that you will lose the ability to feel emotions which could lead one to become a monster, devoid of feelings. There are some symbols that when I use them take on certain colors regardless of how I try to see them. Greel-ya for instance to me seems to be a dark mauve color and Freyl-Tay is pink which could be an objective statement or just a subjective idea on my part. I feel that beyond those symbols with specific colors attached the reader should experiment with different colors and make note of the results. Did it feel different? Did the results change?

The Rún Valdr symbols have the advantage in that they are very specific in scope and do not have the same multi-layer complexity that the runes have. This is simply because I asked for symbols to do specific things. For example, the activation symbols have a very simple purpose of starting the energy flow during a working. There is no other deeper, or hidden meaning behind that. I have to admit that I'm tempted to feel that the runes started out much the same way. A good example is Fehu, which is basically just about wealth. Modern authors have expanded on this idea and have abstracted it to such a great degree that I'm sure the original users would not recognize the meaning anymore. Abstractions are fine, but you need to ask yourself if it helps you come up with a practical way of using the runes in a Rún Valdr working. And yet this same sort of layering is actually happening in Rún Valdr. Naglor, the symbol for migraines turns out to work great for all kinds of pain. Here is an example of new layers of meaning already attaching themselves to a Rún Valdr symbol. I imagine in a hundred years each of these symbols will have multiple meanings much like the runes.

Rún Valdr Symbols

Now we will turn our attention to the symbols that are specific to Rún Valdr beyond the runes themselves. In many ways these symbols are the heart of Rún Valdr and offer the Rún Valdr practitioner many useful tools.

I would like to take a moment to make some comments on the descriptions of the symbols themselves. Some symbols have pages of description, while some have a brief paragraph. The shorter descriptions are usually due to that symbol having a very specific task that doesn't need all that much elaboration. Sometimes it's because while I may have received the symbol, I've not used it very much so have not really dug deep into all that can be done with that symbol.

All of the symbols were given to me by my Gods, Odin or Freyja. Sif and Idunna contributed some as well.

Shai Nal - Power Increase

Pronunciation: Shigh-Nahl

Shai Nal is the most important of the Rún Valdr symbols, and it is the keystone of the whole system. It was the first symbol I got from Freyja and was for increasing one's power. It was described as "bringing the iron within." The image of the symbol gives a bit of a clue to its purpose. The energy moves down the line and is concentrated at the dot.

Shai Nal is central to Rún Valdr in several ways. The first is in how Shai Nal is used in Rún Valdr workings. More will be touched on in the section on workings, but to be brief, one programs Shai Nal with various runes and symbols specific to your need and then lets the program run. Thus a practitioner only needs to concentrate on maintaining the image of Shai Nal during a working. Shai Nal's relatively simple shape makes this fairly easy to do. When I say that Shai Nal is programmed, I mean that the other runes or symbols chosen for any particular working are sent into, or merged, so that Shai Nal is loaded with the qualities of the rune or symbol. It is this programming of Shai Nal that allows the practitioner to just concentrate on Shai Nal by itself rather than trying to deal with the multitude of runes and symbols together which would be mentally taxing.

Shai Nal may be used by itself to help increase one's personal power and to help acclimatize oneself to the energies used in Rún Valdr. After a Rún Valdr workshop, I had a fellow come up to me complaining that he was having a bad reaction to the attunement. He had developed a very bad headache suddenly and figured that the attunement was the cause. I instructed him to meditate on Shai Nal and see how things worked out. My reasoning was that Shai Nal's inherent purpose is to increase and manifest power so that by using the symbol on its own one should gain a greater degree of capacity for the Rún Valdr energy. I'm happy to report that later he said my idea worked and that he felt much better.

I would recommend everyone to meditate on Shai Nal on a regular basis, especially in the early days of learning Rún Valdr. It will not only help one become accustomed to Rún Valdr energies, but will help increase one's own power. The more you use it, the stronger you will become. I recall my early days with Reiki, before I had my first attunement. My teachers had regular healing circles where they would discuss Reiki and then work on the participants. I noticed right away that their hands would get very hot, almost burning. However at the time I had my second level Reiki attunement I noticed that their hands were no longer hot, although I could feel the energy moving within me. I likened the experience to electricity flowing through wires. If the wire is very small, then it will heat up quickly when a strong current is passed through it. However with higher gauge wire, the less heat there will be as the resistance drops. The same thing, I figure, can happen with people as well. Before I could do Reiki, my resistance was high and thus my instructor's hands felt hot. As I got more and more attunements, my resistance decreased and so the energy no longer felt hot.

I feel that working with Shai Nal on a regular basis acts to increase our own energy wire gauge so that we can handle greater amounts of energy. The original reason I got the symbol was a way to increase my own power. It just so happened to work well as a focus for Rún Valdr workings. I would recommend using Shai Nal with the color Gold. It was mentioned to me by Odin that one should not see it as black. It will still work, but will strip away one's emotions and that is not good. This is not a suppression of emotions, but robs one of the ability to feel emotions.

Terra Nal - Translated Shai Nal

Pronunciation: Terra-Nahl

I got this from Odin after the incident mentioned below.

Terra Nal came about after having a brief discussion at a Pagan convention, ConVocation (located in Michigan), with Michelle Belanger, the famous psychic vampire and author of (among others) the Psychic Vampire Codex and the Energy Codex. Psychic vampires are people who have a hard time generating their own energy to sustain their bodies, and must take it from others, whether subconsciously, or consciously. While standing in a hallway discussing psychic vampires I had mentioned that my Reiki teachers had instructed me to just turn on Reiki energy if I was ever attacked by a psychic vampire (meaning that one started sucking away my energy without my permission). However, Michelle, who happened to be passing by, mentioned that Reiki, and perhaps other energy such as found in Rún Valdr is not necessarily compatible with psychic vampires, that it was not really the kind of energy easily used by the human body in that way. She also mentioned an acquaintance of hers that would run Reiki or other energy, translate it within herself to then pass it on. This got me to thinking that it would be fairly easy to get a symbol that would do the work of translating this energy into a form more compatible with the human body. Not only would this make things easier for any psychic vampire learning Rún Valdr, but I would imagine it would also help with any healing working as the energy would be easier for the body to use directly.

Terra Nal can be used in place of Shai Nal for those times when energy more compatible for a body to utilize is needed, such as with a healing or feeding a psychic vampire. The value of this symbol is that it will automatically translate the energy into the more palatable form when the working is activated. Otherwise it is used in the same manner as Shai Nal.

Shambul - Activation (working)

Pronunciation: Shahm-bool.

This symbol came from Odin.

Shambul is another key symbol. After Shai Nal is programmed, Shambul is used to start the working. It is like flipping a switch to let the energy run through the program. Shambul is unusual in that it is not concentrated on like Shai Nal, nor is it loaded into Shai Nal like other symbols and runes. It is briefly pictured, long enough to activate the working (by saying Shambul's name mentally, with force) and then the image is let go. It is used much like the match that briefly flares to light a candle and is then blown out and discarded. However, the effect of the match on the candle is long lasting. It is similar with a Rún Valdr working. Once Shambul is used, the energy starts flowing and one merely needs to keep concentrating on Shai Nal to keep the energy flowing.

The idea for Shambul comes fairly directly from Reiki's Power Symbol taught at the second level attunement although I think there are some differences. In Reiki, the Power Symbol is used to connect one to the Reiki energy so that it can flow through you. With Rún Valdr Shambul taps into a more universal and generic source of energy. The two analogies sound rather similar, but I feel there is a distinction. Reiki makes a connection to a specific healing energy that seems to have its own consciousness and awareness. In Reiki, the Reiki energy really does all the work. However, in Rún Valdr I see it as being more mechanical in nature. You still connect to some vast field of energy, but I don't really see it as having an awareness of its own. It is merely a source of energy for one to use as they see fit, you are in control of what the energy does, not the energy source.

Rún Valdr has several different symbols that act like Shambul and each will be discussed in turn. Why so many one may ask? I have a theory and it relates to safeguards and the Rún Valdr system. A lot is made of Reiki being extremely safe and having lots of safeguards built into it so that it can't be abused and hurt others. Folks have found that it can, indeed, be abused, but you have to work hard to do so. Just using Reiki by itself won't harm the patient or the person doing a healing. Overall Reiki is as safe as everyone says it is. However, I don't think that Rún Valdr has very many safeguards built into it at all. It is much more "raw" and leaves whether to help or hurt up to the individual practitioner. That said, my theory goes along the lines that any safeguards are built into the activation symbols. You could say that Shambul is fairly tame. Other activation symbols may not be, as they seem to be stronger, or deeper, than others. You can look at each activation symbol and see them as giving access to the same basic energy source but at different levels of intensity and output. Sometimes you may want more or less energy for any given need. Work on young children may require a lighter tough than trying to avert a hurricane.

Also to be fair, in my search for more and more power, I have experimented with symbols that give a greater and greater output of energy. This is another, and more truthful, reason why there are different activation symbols. I wanted to be stronger in my use of Rún Valdr, to be more effective. Rún Valdr is a search for power, and it should be repeated that it is not a healing system but a magical system that can, as a by-product, be used for healing.

Vash Tul - stronger Shambul symbol.

Pronunciation: Vahsh-Tool

I'm not sure anymore where this symbol came from. Most likely it was from Odin. Sometimes, in the early days, I would just pray for a symbol and draw what I was inspired to draw.

Vash Tul is an attempt to squeeze more power out of the system based on the premise that the power symbol limits the amount of energy traveling through a working. So I asked for a stronger activation symbol to have access to more energy. Vash Tul has a definite different feeling to it when compared to Shambul. When I use Vash Tul, the energy flow is more intense in nature and supplies a greater amount of energy flow than when using Shambul.

Dorva - Channeling Energy

Pronunciation: Dor-Vah

I received this symbol from Odin.

This symbol was first received to channel energy with an eye towards channeling Deities. I figured a good symbol to help the Deity enter the human body would be beneficial. While I never really got going with the whole channeling thing, I found that Dorva also acts as a good activation symbol that, to me at least, seems definitely stronger than Shambul. This symbol was a favorite to use as an activation symbol for a long time until Valtor came along. I just really liked the feel of it.

Valtor - Even stronger Shambul symbol

Pronunciation: Val-Tor

This symbol came from Odin.

In exploring the idea that different activation symbols could have different strengths, I asked for an even stronger activation symbol and got Valtor. This symbol is quite strong compared to Shambul. There is a distinct difference in the feeling and energy flow between Shambul, Vash Tul, Dorva and Valtor. It is worth experimenting to see which works best for you in different circumstances.

If you use each of the different activation symbols you will notice that each has a different feel and energy output.

Reloxon - Distance (Time & Space) - Color is white

Pronunciation: Reh-Lox-On

This symbol came from both Odin and Freyja. A lot of the symbols that mimic Reiki symbols were gained by visiting both Odin and Freyja together.

Reloxon was received at a direct request by myself to get a symbol that could traverse both time and space as the Reiki distance symbol did. And as mentioned elsewhere, Reloxon is a much simpler symbol then the Reiki distance symbol.

If you are using it for a distance working the easiest way to use Reloxon is to see yourself inside one of the circles and the target person/place/thing in the other end. Then do the symbol activation and you are now connected. The size of each circle does not need to be seen as the same size relative to each other. If you are in one circle, the other could by connected to another person, or to a house, or to a mountain, etc. Each circle can be as big or small as needed.

Reloxon is one of the few symbols that can be used by itself outside of a working. It covers time as well as space. The most obvious application is to program a working now but have it take effect at some future time. For example say it is Saturday and you learn that your friend is having surgery next Tuesday. You may be at work during the surgery or otherwise busy and would not be available to do a working then. You can connect to the person now, on Saturday, using Reloxon with the intent that it is connecting during the time of the surgery on Tuesday. Then do the working as normal safe in the knowledge that the energy will be received when needed. More will be mentioned about distance workings in the next chapter.

I have also used Reloxon when doing distance attunements and workings. This is vital if you want to connect to someone for an attunement or working and there is no way to actually physically be in the same room. However it has other uses. In particular there have been times when an attunement has been scheduled for x o'clock, but for some reason I missed the appointed time. I was able to use Reloxon to make sure the person got their attunement when they were expecting it. Again intention plays a big part. I used Reloxon to have a distance attunement to start for a person at 5pm. However he received it at 4pm. I had assumed he was in the same time zone as me, but he was actually an hour behind.

Reloxon can also be used to program a working to last for a specific amount of time after you stop. Say a friend has a bad toothache and can't see the dentist until tomorrow. You can do a working to help with the pain, but before you end, use Reloxon with the intent that it keep working until after they can see the dentist. I tend to see one end of Reloxon in the "now" and the other end at the future ending time. You would then instruct the working to continue working on its own until the required ending time. This capability is highly useful in any number of situations.

Reloxon can also be used to do multiple workings or attunements. That is you can do workings or attunements on a group of people all at once rather than doing them one at a time. Basically you use multiple Reloxon symbols connecting yourself to multiple people when doing a working or attunement. This is a big time saver if you are teaching a class to a group and only have a short amount of time. Doing one attunement that affects everyone at once is shorter than doing fifty individual attunements.

This is a very flexible and powerful symbol that has many uses. I also cannot say enough how great it is that the symbol is so simple compared to the very complex Reiki one.

Reloxoné - Energy Channel - Color is purple

Pronunciation: Reh-Lox-Ahnay.

I received this symbol from Odin.

Reloxoné looks very similar to Reloxon and differs in two ways. First the color is purple instead of white. Also there is an added é at the end of the name, which changes the pronunciation of the symbol. Reloxoné came about as a way to power magical objects. I wanted to be able to connect them to a power source, like the sun, earth, moon, another galaxy, elemental planes, etc so that they would be self-powered and would not need to be charged all the time. Reloxoné is used much in the same way as Reloxon, but the intent is not to just connect two things, but to create a conduit between the two. This conduit can be one-way or two-way depending on the intent. For the purposes of powering an object the conduit could be one-way or two-way (like a circuit) from the power source to the object. I have found two-way works really well.

Reloxoné was great in allowing an object to have access to an energy source to power its programming. Over time I noticed that objects would still lose their charge regardless. After contacting Odin, I received a different symbol to use as a permanent conduit (See Relanor below). Reloxon remains a very viable symbol to use during workings. Since Reloxoné does not create a permanent energy conduit or channel, it can be used during a working to add extra energy from an appropriate energy source and then dispersed after it is no longer needed.

To use Reloxoné to add extra energy during a working you would see the active Shai Nal in one end and the power source in the other end. Do the symbol activation and you will be connected. I like to use Dorva to initiate the energy movement in the conduit you have created, as Dorva's main function is to channel energy. Use your intention that the conduit be one way or two way from the power source to the working. You may also use Lugar to open up the conduit more to allow greater energy to pass through the channel. This symbol can be used between people to create a two-way conduit between them. This can range from sharing energy, feelings, thoughts, etc. One's imagination is the only limit. I suppose it could be used as a one-way conduit as well, so that a healthy person could give energy to someone who's weaker, for example to help someone during a physical ordeal (race, marathon, child birth, etc) or if they are lost in the wilderness and hurt waiting for rescue.

Again intent plays a very important part when using Reloxané.

 **Relanor - Permanent Energy Channel - Color is bright blue**

Pronunciation: Rel-ahnor

I received this symbol from Odin.

Relanor was developed after the problem mentioned above of the magical objects I created losing their energy. At first Reloxoné worked, but this was not enough as it was only a temporary conduit.

Upon meditating, Odin gave me Relanor to use. It acts much like Reloxoné, however, it is a permanent conduit rather than a temporary one. This makes it ideal to use to power magical objects, even servitors.

Relanor is used similarly as Reloxoné except that you are creating a permanent conduit to a power source rather than a temporary one. Besides using it on objects I've experimented with using it on each of my chakras to give them a boost. When using Relanor, intention is very important, especially in terms of creating a one-way conduit (from a power source to a chosen object) or a two-way conduit. For a long time I thought that when creating self-powered magical items you will want to create a one-way conduit so that energy flows from the energy source into the object. However I have found that a two-way conduit is more effective. In electricity, you need the return flow so that the energy can travel properly in a circuit. I've noticed better results with two-way conduits for objects rather than a one-way conduit which may hamper the flow of energy..

Because Relanor creates a permanent power conduit I would suggest caution if one plans on using it between two people. It is really designed to be used on inanimate objects, but there is no reason why it can't be used with people or pets. One must be very clear if creating a permanent conduit is a good idea, and of course, permission and full consent should be gained from both sides. This can be used to really inconvenience someone if a one-way conduit was created to drain someone of energy. Or conversely to feed energy/influence to someone as an attempt to control them. And because it is permanent it's not like you can just turn it off if it becomes inconvenient. For most cases the temporary Reloxoné would be sufficient.

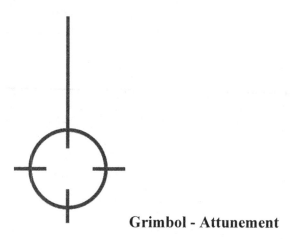

Grimbol - Attunement

Pronunciation: Grim-bohl

I received this symbol from Odin when He showed me how to do attunements.

There are two Grimbol symbols. One to attune living things and one to attune objects. Much like the attunement symbol in Reiki, this symbol is the method for giving an attunement to someone, or something, making it one of the major symbols in Rún Valdr. It should be repeated that there is only one attunement for Rún Valdr unlike Reiki which has three separate attunements, one for each of the three levels. There is only one level in Rún Valdr. I have found that unlike Reiki attunements I actually get energetic feedback during a Rún Valdr attunement. Usually this is a tingling in my palm. In giving Reiki attunements you don't feel anything, energetically. You go through the motions and fabulous results happen, but you don't feel a thing. I was pleased with Rún Valdr attunements that there was a definite feedback to the process. I could sense if I could speed up, or if I should slow things down. Sometimes things felt very slick and fast, other times I could feel resistance, and knew to slow down.

The Grimbol symbol for giving attunements to objects came about because objects I had attuned were losing their charge. In addition to gaining Relanor, Odin suggested a new attunement symbol just for object and thus was born the second symbol. This symbol will be discussed further below. Detailed instructions on giving attunements will be given in a later chapter.

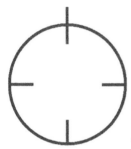 **Tunai - Sealing**

Pronunciation: Too-Nigh

This symbol was received from Odin. There may have been input from Freyja.

Tunai was needed to seal the attunement. In Reiki there is not a specific sealing symbol to cap off an attunement. One uses the Power Symbol instead (or at least that's what I was taught). I felt having a separate symbol for this was important. Tunai is also very useful to use when ending a working or even a meditation.

I've had a student say that during a working their crown chakra was opened, and then after using Tunai the crown chakra closed and returned to a normal state. Needless to say, Tunai should be used after each working andor attunement without fail.

Jutanhowr - Grounding

Pronunciation: Yoo-tan-How-er

I'm not sure who specifically gave me this symbol. Perhaps both Odin and Freyja.

There is a nice symbol from Karuna Reiki that is really great at grounding. It puts one's energy and body back to a normal grounded state. I wanted something that acted like that symbol and Jutanhowr was the result. Jutanhowr work pretty quickly and can be used by itself without bothering with Shai Nal. I've used it with great results as various festivals where there might be a lot of energy work going on and people had need of grounding.

Lugar - Opening/Closing

Pronunciation: Loo-Gar

Again I'm not sure who specifically gave me this symbol.

My Reiki teachers had a symbol for opening and closing the aura that was part of their first level Reiki teaching. This was to help with energetic interactions. Combined with ADF's ritual use of opening and closing Portals to the other realms got me thinking. It would be nice to have a symbol that could be used for any sort of opening and closing. Lugar was the symbol that was given. In ADF druid rituals, a big part of the ritual is to open Portals to the Other realms so that interaction with the Kindred (Ancestors, Nature Spirits, and the Gods) is easier and more effective. I've used this symbol a lot during ADF rites to open and close the Portals and it works great. It could also be used for any other type of opening or closing, such as an energy blockage, open a path for yourself, close down something like a relationship, or a negative energy connection with someone. I suppose it could be used for pain management for closing down the pain, or the sensation of pain.

I have used it to help open up sinuses on people with sinus pressure, and it worked fine. I'm sure it could be used for asthma to open up the bronchia. Also since allergic reactions are an immune overreaction, perhaps closing it down could help with allergies. This symbol can be used for any purpose where opening or closing can help, Again, since you have one symbol to do both opening and closing, your intentions are important. I also like to use a bit of imagery of the symbol growing larger for openings or shrinking for closings.

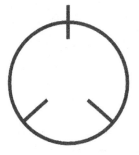

Idunnath - Restoration

Pronunciation: Idoon-nath

I received this symbol from the Goddess Idunna, I believe.

Working with the Goddess Idunna has given me an appreciation for restoration. This symbol is designed to help restore things to their original state. Whether you are tired, sick, or just worn out it should help you recover. I supposed it could be used for non physical things like restoring relationships or even one's emotions or soul, especially during those times when you feel just soul-sick and "dead" inside. It may even be affective for mental problems as well. Regardless, this symbol is good to use for any kind of healing work.

Jorum - Regeneration

Pronunciation: Jor-um – This is one of the only symbols where the "J" has a hard J sound rather than a Y sound.

This symbol may have been received from either Freyja or Idunna.

Similar to Idunnath, this symbol represents more physical regeneration. Healing quickly, etc. Again think superhero powers like Wolverine's regenerative abilities. Not that this symbol will give you that kind of healing ability, but it's a step in the right direction. This would be good to use after any sort of injury, or if you stay up too late and know you won't get a proper amount of sleep. This symbol is especially good when working with Idunnath.

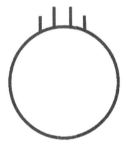 **Grija - Purification - Color is white**

Pronunciation: Gree-Yah

I received this symbol from Freyja.

Grija was another early symbol from Freyja and focuses on purification. Even the symbol itself rather resembles a cauldron with steam rising above it. I like to see this as burning away impurities, or at least a refining kind of action. It can be used for any kind of purification need from purifying a space to purifying the self.

I find that when using this upon myself I become much more prone to developing diarrhea or having to urinate a lot. I suppose it could be said that this is a form of purification in and of itself.

However please experiment on your own as your results may vary from mine. Since our modern society is prone to a lot of toxins, from automobile and industry exhaust to artificial ingredients in our food we can benefit from purification and detoxification. Also can be used to help with poison ivy like reactions. I also imagine it could be used for spiritual purification or any other kind of purification.

Han-So - Transformation

Pronunciation: Hahn-So

I believe I received this symbol from Freyja.

Han-So use to be a much more important symbol in my mind than it is now. It is transformation and my instructions on the quick instructional sheet said to use it every time one did a working. While I still feel that the idea of transformation is very important it is not a huge driving need for me any longer. That said I would still recommend frequent use of this symbol as it is usually easier to transform something than to create something from scratch. Transformation can take many forms and I see this symbol as useful for any sort of transformation required in one's life. One could transform negative energy into positive, transform depression to happiness, even change someone's mind about something. This is one of those symbols that is limited only by your imagination and I think I have only scratched its surface in terms of its capabilities. This is one symbol that I feel I should have done more with as it seems it can be very useful in a wide variety of situations.

 **Gramva - Energy Translation**

Pronunciation: Gram-vah

I got this symbol from both Odin and Freyja.

This is an interesting symbol and its origin is shared with Terra Nal and the same conversation with psychic vampire Michelle Bellenger. My first idea was to create a symbol that could be used during a working to convert the Rún Valdr energy into a form more palatable for psychic vampires. Later I got the idea to have a whole Shai Nal like symbol that automatically translated the energy in the way I wanted. This symbol makes it easier to use the different Shai Nal like symbols instead of always being locked into using Terra Nal. In any case this symbol is handy to use when doing any healing or other work on a person. Since it translates the energy into a form that is more digestible to the body it would work better with the body for any healing

Grishtor - To make holy - Color is gold

Pronunciation: Grish-Tor

I received this symbol from both Odin and Freyja. It kind of looks like a Brigid's cross, or a modified swastika, which for the Northern people (and may other cultures) is a very holy symbol.

I really like this symbol and am really proud of it. The purpose of this symbol is to hallow things, or to make them holy. Thus it is great to use to attune one's religious tools and items or to consecrate an area where ritual or other devotional acts will be performed. I have found that negative entities do not like this energy. So it can be good warding a place or person, or even an object that has attracted the attention of any negative entity. If you are using this symbol and people do not like it I would think that this is an indication of that person being in contact with negative things. I'll go into this a bit later in the book. Suffice to say for now that negative entities don't like this symbol or the energy that it gives off.

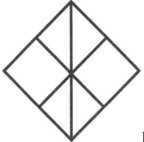

Koltai - Ultimate Protection

Pronunciation: Kohl-Tigh

I'm not sure where this symbol came from. It may be one that I felt compelled to draw and found the meaning later.

This symbol was an attempt at a catch-all type of protection. It seems to work out just fine and I would recommend using in any situation where you feel you need protection. Or as part of a warding in general. Attune your car or house even. It can be used in conjunction with other protection runes.

Unfortunately this is another symbol I have not done much with. It would seem that it would have a lot of value. In the previous chapter there are three runes that have protective qualities: Thurisaz, Hagalaz, and Algiz. Each of these runes protect in different ways. Thurisaz is active defense, hit first before you are hit. Hagalaz is more tricky in that using is it saying, "Lightning has struck here already, and since lightning can't strike twice, bad stuff can't come here. Algiz is more passive protection being more of a barrier that will hurt those who try to get through. Looking at Koltai, it would seem to enclose the thing to be protected. Inside it is the Younger Futhark version of Hagalaz, so maybe that is a clue to how it works. Maybe it is a combination of protections. I would love for people to delve into this symbol and send me feedback on it.

 **Naglor - Migraines/Pain management - Color is dark blue**

Pronunciation: Nag-Lor

I believe this was received from both Odin and Freyja.

This is a very interesting and useful symbol. I grew up suffering from migraines starting as a young child and I know firsthand how devastating they can be. I thought having a symbol to combat migraines would be a good service to these who still get them. Not only is this symbol good with migraines, but it is also freakishly good for dealing with any kind of pain. I had the occasion to use it on someone who had just broken their collar bone. We were camping and I'm not sure if they were able to get his pain meds prescription filled, although the bone was set at a hospital. When I used this symbol the relief was pretty immediate. I was told that I should be called "Vicodin."

This is an example of a symbol having multiple uses that was not intended from the start. I'm also pleased at how useful this symbol is in a practical way. This symbol also looks like a symbol called a

Wolf Hook although I have no idea what this similarity could mean. Having seen the many layers built up over time with the runes, it is nice to see a Rún Valdr symbol start to gain different layers as well.

Roween - Relaxation

Pronunciation: Roh-Ween

I believe this symbol came from Freyja.

This symbol represents not only physical relaxation, but also mental. In our hurried, rushed lives it can be hard to just relax. I myself have a hard time relaxing, since I'm fairly kinesthetic and tend to hold things in my body. When watching boxing I would always find myself twitching as the boxers hit each other. I always find myself physically tense so have to consciously force myself to relax. I thought having a symbol could help as I could then program my chair to send out relaxing energy.

I think this symbol would be good if used as part of a magical item. Attuning one's chair or bed to this would give continuous benefits. Or perhaps a ring or some other item that is worn would work as well.

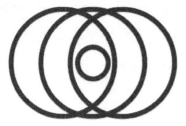

Freyl-Tay - Love

Pronunciation: Frail-Tay

Freyja gave me this symbol without me asking for it. It represents love of all kinds. I haven't really explored using this symbol very much. I suppose it is general enough to be used in most workings on people. Everyone needs love after all. I can see Freyl-Tay being used in working for relationships or for grief issues or just when you need to feel loved.

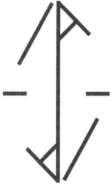

Korgon - For depression/bi-polar - Color is blue

Pronunciation: Kor-Gon

I'm not sure where this symbol came from. Most likely from both Odin and Freyja.

Being depressed can be very painful, and being bi-polar can be equally as bad. This symbol is to be used to help with this kind of problems. To be honest I've not used this much myself. But I encourage experimentation with this symbol

Vornalah - For self-esteem

Pronunciation: Vor-Nah-Lah

I believe this symbol came from Freyja.

I figure that most people suffer from some sort of lack of self-esteem. This symbol was received to give people a tool to help combat this. I would say that it is good to use in most healing type workings.

Haxo - Awakening life in objects

Pronunciation: Hax-oh

I received this symbol from Odin.

There is a Seichim Reiki symbol that awakens life in objects that I thought was pretty cool and wanted for my Rún Valdr system. The idea is that if an object is awake and "alive" it will fulfill its purpose better as it is more aware of what it's doing. I would use this symbol first when creating any magical object, using an activation symbol to get it going.

Haxon - Awakening awareness in animals

Pronunciation: Hax-on

I received this symbol from Odin.

After I asked for Haxo from Odin, He then said to me, "Now here's one for animals." This was a surprise to me as I hadn't thought to ask for anything like this. Its use is still a bit of puzzlement to me. I suppose if used on very young animals on a regular basis you could increase their intelligence. At the very least it would make the animal much easier to train. On the more extreme end it could eventually lead to that species' self-awareness. It is said that animals such as cats and dogs by their close proximity to humans are becoming more and more self-aware so that eventually they will achieve true sentience. This symbol may help speed up the process.

The next five symbols are object specific and typically meant to be used only with objects rather than people

Grimbol - Attunement (for objects)

Pronuciation: Grim-bahl

I received this symbol from Odin.

This symbol works exactly like the other Grimbol attunement symbol, except that it is designed to work with objects rather than people. It is distinguished from the other symbol by a couple of extra lines. This symbol was sought in an attempt to make better magical objects. I had noticed that objects attuned would lose their charge. I went to Odin and received a few tricks. The first was Relanor, and then I obtained this new attunement symbol, and finally Turan for sealing attunements for objects.

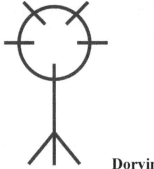

Dorvin - Energy battery

Pronunciation: Dor-vin

I received this symbol from Odin.

This is an object specific symbol, although I suppose it could be used on people. The main idea behind this symbol is to make the object you use it on into an energy battery. Thus the object could collect a large amount of energy which it would then use to fulfill its purpose. If used on oneself, you could give yourself extra reserves of energy to draw upon. Perhaps making each cell in your body into little energy batteries. Especially effective with the chakras, I'm guessing.

Naglaish - Concentrating energy

Pronunciation: Nag-lay-ish

I received this symbol from Odin.

Naglaish is another object specific symbol meant to be used in conjunction with Dorvin. While Dorvin acts as a battery, storing energy, Naglaish takes that energy and concentrates it thus allowing even more energy to be stored and to add potency to any magical item you make. It kind of acts as a capacitor.

Kremen - Radiating energy outward

Pronunciation: Kreh-men

I got this symbol from both Odin and Freyja.

This is another object specific symbol designed to allow your magic item to transmit or radiate its energy outwards to affect things around it, even things at a distance. I sought this symbol because I wanted to make sure that any energy being generated by an object wasn't just locked up in that object. I wanted it to be able to get out and do its job. This symbol should almost always be used with any magical object you make.

Turan - Sealing for objects

Pronunciation: Tur-rahn

Turan is a very important symbol, especially for making magical objects. It is used similar to Tunai, but when doing attunements for objects. This sets the attunement, making it permanent.

Greel-ya - Astral Projection

Pronunciation: Greel-ya

This symbol was given to me by Freyja without my asking for it.

The symbol itself appears to represent a point of intersection between two things, perhaps the physical realm and the astral realm. It is to be used to aid any astral projection or attempts to leave the body. This symbol still remains something of a mystery to me and I'm still looking for the best way to make use of it. I tend to use it before any attempt to make mental journeys to visit my Deities. Or in groups where a guided meditation is being done I will use Greel-ya over the entire group to help them have a stronger experience. I think the best way is to use it as part of an object attunement to create an item to help with astral projection or trance journey work.

Tormal - Burning Fat/weight loss

Pronunciation: Tor-Mahl

I received this symbol from both Odin and Freyja.

This is the second of such symbols. The first one didn't seem to do much of anything. This one is geared towards helping you burn away any extra fat you might have. When using this symbol I have had experiences of not being as hungry or feeling full much earlier that without using the symbol. Again this is one where I encourage people to experiment in using it. I have also found it useful when using this symbol during a working to visualize how you want to look.

Tormaan - Meditative aid

Pronunciation: Tor-Mahn

I received this symbol from Seidh, a Chieftain of Freyja.

This symbol is to be used to still and focus the mind to help when one is meditating or going on trance journeys. The shape very much seems to lock one into a focus. I would use it either by itself like a mandala, or as part of an object designed to help you achieve a trance state.

Symbols and the runes form a very important part of Rún Valdr usage. There are many symbols in this system, much more than any Reiki system that I know of. And these are only the symbols that I am willing to share at the moment. That said, there are actually some experimental symbols that will be shared in a later chapter. They are symbols that have the potential to be very useful, but aren't quite ready to be considered part of the canon of symbols. I do encourage people to visit Odin and Freyja and ask for symbols of your own.

Chapter Four
Using the System

Now that we have learned a bit about the symbols of Rún Valdr it is time to go into detail regarding how to use the system. First we will discuss doing a working on another person, and then we will move on to cover more general magical uses of the system. Even though the technique being taught here focuses on healing, it will be repeated that Rún Valdr is a magical system rather than a healing system. It can be used for healing, but should never be limited to just healing.

Rún Valdr is both simple and complicated in how the system works. If you are used to Reiki, you may be disappointed at the amount of work you will have to do. But this actually means that you have a greater versatility and control over the energy flow of the working. As mentioned earlier, Rún Valdr is not a passive system. So while you are required to do more work, the reward of greater control makes it well worth the effort.

The term "working" is used to describe active Rún Valdr use. For example, "I am going to begin my working now." This is a general term that can be used whether you are doing magic to get a new job, or to heal someone, or to meditate.

Rún Valdr is a very second chakra oriented system. Here is a diagram showing a figure and the general location of the second chakra

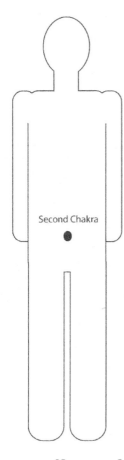

Second Chakra

The first thing you need to understand about how Rún Valdr works is how very important Shai Nal is. Shai Nal is the key to the entire system. This fact cannot be stressed enough. Almost everything you will do centers on programming, activating, and maintaining concentration on Shai Nal. This method, while seemingly complex, actually lets you simplify what you do so as to not tax your concentration too much.

The second key to Rún Valdr is that you need to maintain concentration on your visualization of Shai Nal during your working. Visualization as a whole is quite important in Rún Valdr. I am a very visual person and thus the system that I received from Odin and Freyja ended up being very visually oriented. That's just how the information was translated through me and I apologize to those who have trouble with visualization.

However, I will also add that if you have ever daydreamed or remembered seeing something you have visualized, then you can use this system. No one expects you to "visualize" something so well that it is as though you were actually seeing it with your physical eyes. Almost no one can do that. As long as you can be aware of something in your mind's eye, you are doing it properly.

I find that when one is accessing information from a non-physical place, everything is filtered through one's own mind and subconscious. It's hard to get really objective, direct information, especially when you are going on mental journeys. It is a limitation one must deal with. I feel when making such journeys, it is helpful to be part of a group. That way any overlapping information can be seen as being more objective than any tangential images or information that might come through. Although, if what you bring back works then that is validation too.

Having to maintain concentration during a working is both a boon and a bane. On one hand it can be tedious having to keep up the required concentration. If your concentration falters, you will lose the energy connection and have to start over. This can be frustrating, especially if one is tired or distracted. Reiki has the advantage that one does not need to direct the energy. You simply turn it on and let it do all the work. You can then have a conversation, watch TV, etc, all the while having the Reiki energy doing its thing. It's easy and almost mindless.

On the other hand, maintaining focus allows you the flexibility to consciously direct the energy you are channeling, which you normally can't do while practicing Reiki (or at least have a harder time doing). You are in control of the energy at all times with Rún Valdr. You can tell it where to go and what to do. This versatility allows a Rún Valdr Practitioner to move beyond being locked only into healing and enables one to use Rún Valdr for many different purposes.

Preliminary Skills

Before we get into the actual programming method, there are a couple of techniques that one needs to be comfortable with. These are symbol visualization and symbol activation.

Visualizing and working with the symbols is important since they are your main tools. In Reiki you are required to draw out the symbols, while with Rún Valdr you can merely see the symbol as a whole. If you really feel the need to draw out the symbols, there are a few guidelines. Generally you work from left to right and top to bottom. Circles (except for

Grija) are drawn counter-clockwise. However, I just see the whole symbol in the appropriate color and never worry about drawing them out.

Color is another aspect of Rún Valdr that must be considered as discussed in the previous chapter. Except for those with specific colors of course, like Grija or Reloxon feel free to experiment with different colors to see if you get different results. As mentioned before, one should be careful seeing the runes or symbols as black in color. Black would be better for cursing or more negative uses.

After the concept of symbol visualization comes symbol activation and working activation. Symbol activation is the activation of individual symbols or runes so that they can function within a working. Working activation is turning on the entire working to let the program run.

Those who are trained in Reiki will be familiar with both symbol activation and working activation. Symbol activation in Reiki is simply repeating the name of the symbol to yourself three times. This activates each symbol or primes it to do its job. In Rún Valdr you merely have to say the name of the symbol to yourself once, but it should have a certain amount of mental force to it.

It should be noted that symbol activation is not the same as activating a working. It is done to get each symbol actively involved in the working. Activating a working requires the use of an activation symbol. In Reiki there is one, the Power Symbol. In Rún Valdr there are several, depending on your needs. Each symbol used in a working needs to be activated.

Activating a working gets the whole thing running. To activate a working you first program Shai Nal using symbol activation with each symbol or rune you want to use. Then you see the activation symbol over Shai Nal. Say its name to yourself, the energy will start to flow, and then let the image of the activation symbol fade from your mind. It has done its job, much like a light switch that has been flipped and the energy will start flowing. Once the working has been activated you only need to concentrate on Shai Nal and direct the energy.

A word about ethics: Rún Valdr gives you lots of tools to affect people in addition to doing general magical work. It is always best to get permission to work on any individual before doing any work for them. Sometimes this is necessary even when working on oneself. Sometimes people don't want your help and it's their right not to accept it. A formal act of granting permission can be a powerful thing and insures that you don't have to fight the person you are working on during the working.

I have come to the conclusion that it is very important to get permission when doing a working, even when working on oneself. I have noticed when doing a working for myself that there is a lot of buzz or noisy kind of energy. It seems agitated. But when I state that I give myself permission to accept the energy and to accept its changes, then everything calms down and flows very quietly and smoothly. Remember people are complex things and communication with the various parts, including the subconscious can be very beneficial.

You might formally ask anyone you are working on if you have their permission to do the working on them. The same is most likely true for attunements as well. While getting formal permission to do a working is probably not entirely necessary, there isn't any harm and will most likely go a long way towards a good working.

This brings us to curses. Curses are nasty things and I don't recommend doing them if at all possible. Among Rún Valdr practitioners, there has been some heated discussion related to curses. Many don't think they are appropriate under any circumstances, some think you will just end up hurting yourself as much as your victim. Others see it as pointless and a waste of time. I suppose one could see it as a cathartic process if nothing else. I tend to take a more practical approach and see cursing as a tool, like any other tool. Or perhaps weapon would be a better word, like a gun. And with firearms you had better be prepared to accept any consequences for your actions if you use them.

To me curses are much the same way. If there is no other way to deal with a problem you do have the option to curse if you want, need.

Programming Shai Nal.

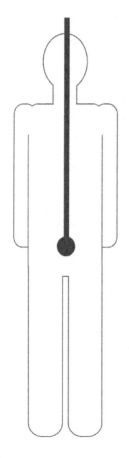

The method is fairly straight forward although there are a few variations. When working on another person, or oneself, I like to see Shai Nal inside the body, the ball part anchored in the second chakra (also known as the hara, or sacral chakra), which is located roughly three fingers widths below your navel. The line part extends a couple inches above the head.

For working on others, I recommend placing both hands on their body. I had started out with the person laying down and placing one hand on the top of the head and the other hand over the second chakra. But that can be read as unprofessional if you don't know the person you are working on. I now tend to just have the person sit while I stand behind them and place my hands on their shoulders. I feel this is less awkward for both parties.

Once you visualize Shai Nal within the person you are working on (or yourself) it is time to program it with runes and/or other symbols. What I like to do is to see the rune or symbol superimposed over Shai Nal. Then I do the symbol activation for it and then see it sink into Shai Nal, which represents the symbol being programmed. I like to visualize Shai Nal glowing briefly to show that the symbol has been programmed into Shai Nal. You can do whatever you like to help you in this process. Anything to more fully engage your senses will help you make the concept real for you is good. You could imagine a sound to signify that the symbol has been programmed into Shai Nal, or a smell, or see a burst of color. It doesn't matter as long as you can firmly feel that each rune or symbol has been properly programmed into Shai Nal.

Realize that you don't have to keep visualizing each rune or symbol after it has been programmed. That is too complicated for anyone without savant type of abilities to manage. The only symbol you need to maintain concentration of is Shai Nal. As each subsequent symbol has been programmed, let it go, knowing that its energies have been incorporated into Shai Nal.

Repeat these steps for each rune or symbol you plan to use.

Activating the Working

Now that all the symbols/runes are programmed into Shai Nal it is time to activate the working. For that you need an activation symbol. Simply visualize the activation symbol (whether it is Shambul, Dorva, Vash Tul or Valtor), large, over Shai Nal and do the symbol activation for the activation symbol. The energy will start to flow and you can let the image of the activation symbol fade away. It is not needed anymore. It acts like a light switch or a lit match to a piece of paper. It just starts the energy flowing. Even though you don't maintain the image of the activation symbol it does release a steady stream of energy that lasts as long as you maintain concentration on Shai Nal.

If your concentration wavers you will lose the energy connection and have to start over. If this happens, I would recommend seeing Shai Nal new and fresh. Re-program it and re-activate the working. This ensures that there is nothing missing from the working if you were to just re-activate it without re-programming. However, feel free to experiment with this to see what is most effective for you.

If you use other activation symbols other than Shambul you will feel a different quality to the energy moving through you. It may feel stronger, or more intense, or even just deeper. I encourage you to try out the various activation symbols and find one that works best for you, or even works best for different kinds of workings you may be doing.

Maintaining the Working

With the energy flowing, maintain concentration and visualization of Shai Nal throughout the entire working. This is a key step. I like to see light coming from Shai Nal which fills the person I'm working on. This gives the intent that the working is affecting the person. Feel the energy fill them up as it works on them.

At this point I like to direct the energy with a sort of internal dialogue. I will tell the energy to go here, or there, to take away pain, to speed up healing, etc. Remember you are in control of the energy and as a natural result, you have the right to tell it what to do. Normally it is simply a matter of saying, "Heal this person. Take away the pain. Knit the bones (heal the cut, remove the headache, bring self-esteem etc., whatever the problem,)." Don't be afraid to tell the energy what you want done and then expect it to do what you ask of it.

Once, while doing a working for a person, I found myself engaged in a sing-song patter, almost like spoken word. For example a simple healing would come out like:

"Send the energy through the body to heal the wounds, heal the wounds. Strengthen the body, make it whole, make it strong, make it bright. Repair the damage and fill the body with light and health. Light and Health. Light and Health. Let the body be strong and whole, filled with the energy of health. Let the body use this energy to be whole and full. Strong, strong, strong… Whole and healthy, whole and healthy, whole and healthy. Healthy and strong as though brand new, whole and strong."

You would keep up this patter for the entire treatment. I found that as time went on, the pattern of the words changed and I could notice changes in the energy and images I was "seeing." It was a wonderful experience for me. It allowed me to work closer with the energy then just saying, "Go here, do that." It was like establishing a relationship with the energy to work in a partnership, not just with the energy, but with the person receiving the energy as well. It allowed a different kind of feedback as the pattern of the words changed.

As you work on someone let yourself be open to various kinds of feedback coming from the person. This can indicate trouble spots, or let you know when you are done and can end the working. For example, the person may seem quite dark, but as the working progresses they grow lighter. When they come all nice and sparkly and light the work is done. Or sometimes you might have the area being worked on change colors, or tonal quality, or any number of types of feedback.

There is one thing that everyone should be aware of. I have heard, from those more sensitive than myself that different people are energetically "wired" differently than others. Some energy workers will see that the energy is flowing strangely and try to shift the energy around into a more "normal" pattern. This can cause even worse problems for the person being worked on. In a way it's kind of like short circuiting electrical wiring. Bad things can happen. So be aware that just because something might look weird, it might be normal for that person. On the other hand it may be out of whack and needs to be adjusted to get back on track. You should talk with the person letting them know what you are sensing. They may need you to leave things the way they are. Never assume that what you are sensing is wrong and needs to be fixed. They may just be different. You can also do a healing working with the intention of doing whatever needs to be done while working with the existing energy pattern of the person you are working on.

Ending the Working

When the working is done you finish by using Tunai, the sealing symbol. Visualize Tunai, large, over the person and do the symbol activation. Then you can drop the visualization of Shai Nal and stop the working. Reiki does not have the same idea when it comes to stopping a working. You go through the hand positions and when you are done with the various positions you are done with the working. I felt quite strongly that with Rún Valdr it is important to seal the working with Tunai, just like you would seal an attunement.

I mentioned, when discussing Tunai, that one student had said that while experiencing a working, her crown chakra was wide open. After the sealing it closed back to a normal state. Other students over the years have echoed this sentiment and that it felt right to use Tunai to end a working.

Distance Workings

By using Reloxon one can do a working at any distance, or even across time. It is this capability that makes this symbol so important and useful. Using Reloxon is easy. Merely visualize each thing or person to be connected in one of the circles and do a symbol activation, saying the name,

Reloxon, to yourself with some mental force. It is that simple. And once you are connected to your target you may then do a working or an attunement as though you were right next to them. When doing distance workings or attunements, I visualize myself doing the normal things I would for a physical working or attunement. I see myself visualizing Shai Nal in the person, programming it with the runes and/or symbols I have chosen to use, etc. Even though all the "action" is being done in my head, I get very real results.

With Reloxon you can do a working or attunement no matter where the target person is. You can even use Reloxon to program to work at a different time or to create a continuing effect. Or say you have only a brief time to do a working on someone with chronic pain issues, perhaps from a broken bone. You can do a working for as much time as you have and then use Reloxon to program the working to continue for however long you desire, as discussed earlier. I like to visualize a time frame with one end of Reloxon at now and the other end at the ending point somewhere in the future. The intention is that the working will continue for the proscribed amount of time. I would say that the longer you have the working last, the less effective it will be and the faster it will degrade. Use your judgment and come up with a reasonable amount of time.

Other Considerations

Some symbols can be used by themselves without using Shai Nal. These are Grishtor, Jutanhowr, Reloxon, Reloxoné, Relanor, Roween, Tormaan, Greel-ya, Koltai and Gar-Lon. These for sure can be used without Shai Nal as has been discussed in Chapter Three (Except for Gar-Lon which is discussed in the Attunement chapter). I encourage experimentation to see if others would work too.

That said I still feel that the best results for most symbols will be in conjunction with Shai Nal, since that symbol's job is to concentrate and manifest energy as well in increasing its strength.

You can also experiment using any symbol by itself and the using one of the activation symbols to start the energy flowing without using Shai Nal.

Since you are free to program Shai Nal with whatever runes or symbols you need, you can see how versatile and flexible Rún Valdr is. It is this versatility that gives it an edge over Reiki, not just for healing, but other applications ranging from changing the weather to getting a job to quitting smoking to protection. Once you have the basics down you can then modify them to fit almost any situation.

For magical work, Reloxon, Reloxoné, and Relanor will be important. I have already discussed the importance of Reloxon in regards to being able to reach out across space and time. Reloxoné and Relanor also have a very important role since they are the means of bringing in energy from various sources; energy that can be used to power your magical workings. Because Reloxoné only creates a temporary conduit, it can safely be used in almost any working. Relanor, which sets up a permanent conduit needs to be used more judiciously. You need to be sure that a permanent conduit is appropriate for whatever you are doing. For creating a magical object, sure. For a simple healing, maybe not.

One example of the use of Reloxoné and Relanor is in attuning one's chakras or even all the cells in the body with a connection (permanent or otherwise) to a strong power source (sun, moon, earth, a distance galaxy, the elemental plane of water, etc.). Thus each chakra or cell in your body is constantly being filled with energy that can be used. Reloxoné is very useful for putting energy anywhere you need it to go no matter where it happens to be.

A Rún Valdr working can be used in a wide variety of purposes. In this chapter I only focused on using it to heal someone, but really there is no limit on how it can be applied. Instead of healing you could be working on helping the person learn a new skill, gain protection, aid with trance work, etc.

The basics of Rún Valdr are quite simple once you get the hang of things and you will find yourself modifying the basic technique to fit many situations in your life or even going free form with it. In the next chapter we will discuss using Rún Valdr for magic and going beyond the basic working model.

Alternative Working Techniques

In addition to doing a full working on someone you also have other methods of using Rún Valdr. For example if someone has an injury, you can work in a localized way. For example, let's say someone cut their finger. You could visualize Shai Nal rather small with the dot part at the wound. You would still program it and activate the working the same way, but you would just be working on the specific area. I've done this many times and it works fine.

I have done some experimenting and using an activation symbol by itself will keep up a stream of energy as long as you maintain concentration on the energy itself. Thus you can do a working without using Shai Nal at all.

If you are used to more traditional energy work you could then get the energy going and then direct the raw energy yourself without having to worry about draining your own resources. This would also be good for a lot of massage therapists who happens to incorporate Reiki in their work. You could just use an activation symbol and add extra energy to the massage session. This method can allow you extra flexibility as to how you want to use the energy. You could even program your hands with symbols, get the energy flowing and then just concentrate on the energy flow, directing the energy. Again, intention would play a critical role.

Another alternative use is to use Reloxoné and attune it for specific purposes. You would set up Reloxoné with a power source as normal with you or your target on the other end. Before using Dorva to initiate the energy flow you would use Grishtor, attuning Reloxoné with the specific symbols you have chosen. You would seal the attunement and then use Dorva to start the energy flow. Thus you have a steady stream of specific energies in an automatic Rún Valdr working. Reloxoné can be programmed for specific time periods like Reloxon. You could also use Relanor as above, but for a permanent working.

Chapter Five
Attunements

In this chapter, we will cover the most magical and satisfying part of Rún Valdr: giving attunements. I'm still amazed after doing so many attunements over the years at how wonderful the experience can be. In just a few minutes you can bestow upon someone an ability they never had before. It is truly remarkable, and yet surprisingly simple to do.

An attunement is an initiation, a catalyst which both connects one to a power greater than what can normally be accessed by the ordinary person, and changes you so that you can better channel and work with this energy. I'm really attracted to attunements in general as I find something very compelling about undergoing a process that enables one to gain abilities that one never had before. Or at least gain a much greater control over any existing abilities one may have.

I am reminded of the Amber books by author Roger Zelazny. In these books the main characters could walk a Pattern as an initiatory, or attunement, process and gain powers to walk through alternate realities. It also gave them access to using the Pattern in magical ways. Of course walking the Pattern was quite the ordeal, unlike the Rún Valdr attunement. The Pattern almost physically rebuilt the person and left an imprint of the Pattern within them. While the Rún Valdr attunement is not that dramatic, it does make definite changes to one's energy.

Tchipakkan, a Rún Valdr practitioner who has taught many people, once came across someone involved in what could only be described as Norse Shamanism. While intrigued by Rún Valdr, he was told by his various spirit guides that he should not get an attunement as it would change his energy in a way that was different from what they were trying to achieve. I find this intriguing for a couple of reasons. First it gives some validation that the Rún Valdr attunement is doing something, making a real change in the recipient. Secondly it tells us that there is more than one way to organize and construct one's energy self for different purposes. I'm interested as to what the differences were between what Rún Valdr does and what the Norse Shaman was receiving. It also makes me wonder if Rún Valdr could be altered to gain different results. Different abilities? Stronger power? What other mysteries lie beneath the surface?

Such stories make me curious about the real nature of our beings. It is obvious to me that we are more than mere flesh and blood. There are many energy systems out there that attempt to describe the human energy body. How accurate are they? I find this idea that people are "wired" differently intriguing. How many ways can people be "wired?" For what purpose? I've even met someone who claimed not to have a second chakra. I didn't think that was possible. I suppose that if there is a possibility for physical deformities, then there can also be energetic ones as well.

To be sure, going through a Reiki or Rún Valdr attunement effects one's energy system. Having myself gone through Reiki training, and later in developing Rún Valdr, I can attest to this. After my second level Reiki attunement, the hands of my teachers no longer felt hot. I feel that attunements such as Reiki and Rún Valdr prepare the body, both physically and energetically to handle the specific incoming energy and to be able to channel it appropriately.

It makes me wonder what one can achieve with the right attunement process. Are there attunements out there that can make one more powerful? More sensitive to energies?

Unlike Reiki attunements, which have three different levels of training and thus require three different attunements, Rún Valdr has only one attunement. After I figured I had enough symbols to make a complete system, I made a trance journey to visit my Patron, Odin, to get the attunement process. When Odin told me that there was only one attunement for the entire system I was rather surprised, having been used to the three attunement process of Reiki. However, despite saving a bit of time it has a way of making the process more profound. A lot of information is imparted to the Rún Valdr student. Not only are recipients able to use the Rún Valdr system, but also to give attunements themselves. Odin showed me how to do an attunement and then gave me an attunement. It felt quite interesting, much different than the physical attunement I was to have later and also much different from any Reiki attunement I'd ever had.

Compared to Reiki attunements, the Rún Valdr attunement is fairly simple and direct. The actual attunement takes only minutes, but has a strong effect on the person receiving the attunement. I would like to point out some differences between Reiki attunements and Rún Valdr attunements, at least from my point of view. When doing Reiki attunements, I never felt anything at all. It was like I was going through the motions physically with nothing happening energetically. However, the person receiving the attunement feels all sorts of wondrous things and lots of energy. During my second level Reiki attunement I could feel where my teacher was in the room as he moved around (my eyes were closed during the process) by the energy he was giving off. I could also feel large amounts of energy coursing through me. I always found it odd that you don't feel anything when giving Reiki attunements when the recipient feels so much. Even my teachers commented on this, so it's not just me.

I find with Rún Valdr attunements, however, there is energy feedback so that I can feel something happening during the attunement. I also get a sense of how easily a person is receiving the attunement and can adjust the speed in which I attune the runes and symbols. It is more interactive than with Reiki attunements. My hand starts to tingle during the attunement and I can feel a definite energetic connection going on.

In Reiki, after one undergoes an attunement, there is a 21 day adjustment period. The attunement sort of opens and cleanses the upper chakras and it takes time for any detritus, so to speak, to work itself out. Many people have various physical manifestations. Not illness per se, but some discomfort. Personally I didn't suffer any ill effects after any of my attunements, but I know of others who have.

The jury is out whether or not Rún Valdr has a similar adjustment period. Some students have said no, others, yes, but it is milder, etc. At least in general, the consensus is that there really isn't an adjustment period, but some have reported something happening, so I should warn you that you may experience something. I have had folks not deal with attunements very well so maybe there is some truth to the adjustment period idea for Rún Valdr. At least I can say that it can vary by the individual.

As mentioned earlier, after an attunement done at Wellspring, an ADF festival, a gentleman came up to me after the class and said that he thought he was having a bad reaction to the attunement and that he had a sudden fierce headache. I thought, "Oh great! That's all I need is to kill someone with an attunement." My second thought was, "Well, I can't really undo it." So I advised him to meditate on Shai Nal as this symbol was designed to increase one's power and should help acclimatize him to the new energy. He came back later to say that it had worked.

I have had many people go through both Reiki and Rún Valdr attunements without any ill effect. I think that some people may be more sensitive to the energy than others and have a stronger reaction to an attunement.

Before the Attunement

I always pass out handouts of the system and symbols to everyone before the attunement. In Reiki this would be a big no-no as all symbols must remain sacred and pure and only shown to students after their attunements. I've never felt a similar need for this with Rún Valdr. I have no problem with prospective students seeing the symbols or seeing how a working is done. I feel that anyone would still need an attunement to get the system to work properly anyway, so for me, it's a moot point.

Handouts are indispensable and provide room for students to take notes as well as giving the students most of the information they need to dive in and start using Rún Valdr. I highly recommend them to anyone teaching a Rún Valdr class.

Speaking of handouts, I find it is vital to have a "teacher's copy" of the symbols. This is essentially all the symbols along with their names all on a single sheet of paper. That way I can use one hand to hold the sheet while the other hand is used for the attunement. Other people make large poster boards with all the symbols on them so they can use both hands during the attunement.

The Rún Valdr Attunement Process

A few words first. You will be using symbol activation on each rune and symbol to be attuned. While you may do this out loud, I prefer to do this silently. Especially as your speed increases you will be able to think the names faster than saying them physically.

During a normal working you need to maintain concentration on Shai Nal. During an attunement, you need to maintain concentration on the attunement symbol Grimbol. This should be kept in mind during the entire attunement from when you first use it until you seal the attunement. Otherwise you will lose the thread of the energy and will probably have to start over.

Step 1

Have the person receiving the attunement sit in a chair and stand behind them. The person should be relaxed and have their arms and legs uncrossed. Jewelry can be worn, but not armor. Tchipakkan, mentioned earlier, found out at a Society of Creative Anachronism gathering that wearing chainmail armor (or any kind of armor, I imagine) will block an

attunement.

During a Reiki attunement all the students would have their eyes closed throughout the whole process. But I find this is unnecessary. The students not receiving the attunement can watch the attunements if they want.

Step 2

Place your dominant hand on top of the person's head. The other hand can be used to hold notes or your teacher's copy.

Either way, you only need one hand on the head during an attunement. If going cheat sheet hands-free it is nice to use the free hand to "guide" each rune and symbol down into the second chakra. This can help one visualize the process and also to show students what's going on during the attunement.

Step 3

Use the attunement symbol Grimbol. See it within the person's body with the circle part centered on their second chakra and the main line running up and extending a few inches above their heads. Visualization of Grimbol must be maintained throughout the entire attunement process. In the handouts I recommend seeing the person become the Grimbol symbol as this would focus the attention on the attunement symbol. However, just visualizing the symbol inside the person is fine, and it is what I usually end up doing.

Step 4

Visualize each rune and symbol above their heads. Use symbol activation to activate each one. Then see the rune or symbol travel down the main line into the circle and become anchored in their second chakra. Do this for each rune and symbol in turn.

This is the longest part of the attunement. Take your time and make sure each symbol is firmly in place within the second chakra. With time and confidence in yourself your speed will increase. I, myself, tend to do attunements at a fast pace, unless the person I'm doing the attunement on requires a slower pace. Others like to go slow and be very deliberate with each rune and symbol.

Include the test symbols below in the attunement. You may also want to include any of the extra symbols in chapter eight as well.

I've heard of someone attuning their Rún Valdr students to each rune/symbol individually, in separate attunements, over a long period of time. Don't do this. Attune the person to all the runes and symbols at the one attunement. There is no need to spread it out over multiple attunements. Let me be very clear. If you are doing this to your students, stop it. If your teacher is doing this, tell them to stop or find another teacher. Either way you are wasting your time.

Step 5

Once all the runes and symbols have been attuned, take a moment to silently give the student affirmations. I will admit that this part I took from Reiki attunements as I rather liked the idea. I find that the affirmations I use change from person to person, perhaps to reflect individual needs.

I tend to say things like, "You are a mighty and powerful Rún Valdr Practitioner. Go forth and do great things. Let the energy flow easily and strongly through you." These are a few examples.

Step 6

Once the affirmations are done it is time to seal the attunement. Use Tunai, seeing it large and surrounding the person being attuned. After the symbol activation I always say, silently, "I now seal this attunement with Divine Power, Divine Will, and Divine Grace, now and forever more!" Then I feel the attunement locking into place, like a deadbolt lock sliding into place.

To recap.

1. Have recipient sit and relax

2. Place dominant hand on recipient's head.

3. Use attunement symbol, Grimbol.

4. Attune all the runes and symbols, having them become fixed in the recipient's second chakra.

5. Give affirmation.

6. Seal the attunement

As you can see the actual attunement process is fairly short and except for having to maintain Grimbol, not very physically demanding at all. But it has profound effects that are long lasting. I find, at least for myself, that it takes a while for the attunement to work itself out after the sealing. The first time I taught Rún Valdr I had one of the students give me an attunement. It was the first time I had had an actual physical attunement since Odin did the initial attunement on me some months before. I could feel the different runes and symbols move down my body and enter my second chakra. I remember feeling this quite clearly and distinctly. I also could feel when the sealing happened as well. Then after the attunement was done I could feel energy spreading out from my second chakra, filling me. This process took some time, perhaps a half hour or so. The Rún Valdr attunement felt quite different from any Reiki attunement I had had in the past. A student later described the experience like a massive data dump.

Even though the attunement process is quite quick, the teaching of the techniques can take much longer. There is a lot of material to cover when teaching Rún Valdr, not just giving the attunement, but teaching what the runes and symbols are for, how to do a working, how to make magical objects, and how to give an attunement. Afterwards, you give students time to practice. I've rarely had as much time as I like to teach and would love to do a full weekend course. Usually I have an hour and a half for the entire thing and have to resort to mass attunements and quick practice sessions.

Distance Attunements

One great thing about Rún Valdr is that you can do attunements over great distances. Much like with distance workings, distance attunements are just as easy and effective. This is quite similar to how distance workings operate with a few changes to accommodate the details of how attunements work. This opens up many more opportunities for a Rún Valdr practitioner to teach others since one is no longer restricted by physical distance. I have had the opportunity to give distance attunements not only in other parts of the United States, but in Canada, the UK, Ukraine, Japan, India, Australia, and the Middle East and many other places as well.

Distance attunements follow the previous steps although there are additional preparations to make. You will be using Reloxon to make a connection with someone first. Similar to doing distance workings, I find the easiest way to use Reloxon is to visualize myself in one circle and the target person in the other circle. Then I say the symbol's name to myself for the symbol activation and *voila* you are now connected across space and time. Again the intent is that this connection will last through out the attunement.

Then, similar to doing a distance working, you merely visualize yourself doing an attunement for the person same as if you were physically near.

Mass Attunements

If I'm teaching a class and I don't have a lot of time, I will do a mass or group, attunement. This attunement attunes everyone all at once. It is similar to doing a mass working.

To do a mass attunement you start by seeing Grimbol, the attunement symbol in front of you. Then use Reloxon to connect it to everyone you are going to attune. You do this by visualizing a separate Reloxon starting from Grimbol and going out to each person. Grimbol then looks like it is in the middle of a big spoked wheel. This can be tricky to keep in one's mind's eye all at once. Intention is important here and you must believe that the attunement will go out to each person without fail.

Then you do the attunement as normal except that you are only concentrating on the Grimbol symbol in front of you rather than on any single person. After all the runes and symbols have been put into Grimbol, seal as normal.

Being able to do a mass attunement is a big time saver, especially if you don't have a lot of time to teach. I've had to teach the entire class in only an hour and a half. Without being able to give a group attunement I never would have had enough time.

Self-Attunements

You can do attunements to yourself, so if you come across a symbol you want to use, or to gain a deeper affinity for you can do an attunement on yourself. The steps are the same as a regular attunement, except that you would see Grimbol inside of you rather than in another person.

Rún Valdr Training

After attuning a person the real work of training begins. The actual attunement takes a few minutes. Training can take many hours. Hopefully when you start to teach you will have more time than I normally get.

A lot of students feel that they can't use the system until they have learned the runes. So they start to learn the runes, stop and then never use Rún Valdr at all. I don't agree with this idea. The handouts list all the runes and symbols with keywords as to what they do. There is no reason to delay in using this system until you have mastered the runes or the many, many symbols that go with Rún Valdr.

I tell my students, if nothing else, start with Shai Nal. Meditate on it daily. Visualize it within you and say its name to yourself and then just feel the energy of the symbol. It is designed to increase your power, to manifest that energy. Even just by itself it can do wonders. In those cases where someone gets a headache (or other negative reactions) after the attunement, using Shai Nal can help the person assimilate the new energies.

The first thing I have the students practice is feeling the flow of the energy. I have each student simply use Shai Nal within themselves and then use Shambul to get the energy flowing. Have them experience this for a minute or so and then finish with Tunai. Then have them experiment with other activation symbols such as Dorva and Vash Tul. Have them compare the energies felt from all the different activation symbols.

After this, it is time to have the students practice doing a working on someone. I have the students break up into groups of two to practice, with someone giving the working and one receiving. Start them with something simple like a basic healing working having them program Shai Nal with Fehu and Uruz and then activating the working. Typically the person receiving the energy is sitting down and the person sending the energy is standing behind them with both hands on the shoulders. Again give them a minute or so at this and then have them end with Tunai. Then have the teams switch sending and receiving roles so that both people get to feel both parts. Get feedback from both those sending energy and those receiving it.

Then, I like to have the students practice distance workings. The pairs separate across the room and repeat the working they just did. This time they will first use Reloxon to connect with their partner before visualizing doing the working. The results should be the same whether the person sending the energy is physically touching the person they are working on or if they are across the room.

The demonstration of performing workings at a distance gives the students an idea of the great potential of Rún Valdr. Once they know that space and time are not obstacles the students can grasp the scope of the tools that have been given to them. It teaches them that there are few limits to hamper what they do.

Once the students have had a chance to practice distance workings it is time to have them practice attunements. Start them physically touching, still in groups of two. When teaching, I only make the students attune each other with the first eight runes. This gives them real practice giving attunements, yet does not overload them with having to attune all the runes and all the symbols. This also saves a great deal of time as the students are quite slow and deliberate when practicing attunements. Eight runes is plenty for them to practice with. Have each person in the pair attune the other, switching to make sure both have the opportunity to give an attunement. Again, get feedback from both people. How did it feel to receive and to give the attunement?

After practicing while physically touching, have them practice distance attunements, much as you did when teaching giving a distance working. Again the results should feel the same whether the person giving the attunement is actually touching the receiver or from across the room.

If you have time you can have the students practice doing multiple workings and multiple attunements. This is fun as the students can gain an even greater experience at how versatile and useful Rún Valdr can be.

And if there still is time then you can move onto how to make magical objects. This can be left to last as it is basically just doing an attunement on an object so that it will begin to automatically channel energy that you specify in a way that is required. More on making magical objects will be covered in a further chapter.

How long you spend on each exercise depends on how much time you have to teach. If you have an hour or so, you have to keep things moving fairly briskly. If you have a whole weekend then you can go at a slower pace and take your time to delve into all the little nuances that goes into a working or an attunement. With longer periods of practice you could have the students do full attunements, or design different kinds of working to try on each other, such as general healing, depression, weight loss, stopping smoking, migraines, or other specific things.

Test Symbols

One other thing I like to do is give the students test symbols. The students are attuned to these symbols, but are not told about them. Near the end of the training they are given the symbols and the names. The students are told to use the symbols within themselves and experience the energy of each one. The goal is to tell you what each symbol does.

I normally start this exercise by passing the symbols around so that everyone can copy them down on their own sheets. They are to draw the symbols and write the names. After this is done they visualize the first symbol inside themselves and do a symbol activation. The students should be given a few minutes to feel the energy of the symbol trying to discern what it does and what it's for. Have the students discuss their thoughts on the symbol. After everyone has had a chance to contribute, tell them what the symbol really does.

Repeat this for each of the symbols. I find that very few students are very accurate about the symbols. Occasionally one or two will be spot on while some are vaguely close. It's rather fun to hear all the different thoughts on the symbols. But there is the purpose to this exercise besides being sadistic. It helps the students use the symbols in a different way. It shows them that they can explore the energy within each symbol to become more in touch with that symbol. Also, while I'm convinced you get more from the individual symbols by using them in conjunction with Shai Nal, I feel that it is also valid to just use the symbols by themselves.

The test symbols are :

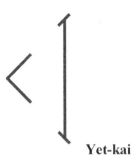

Yet-kai

Yet-kai is for warding a property. Think of it as protection for a place rather than for a person. Koltai is great for protection, but Yet-kai is geared to defending a specific area. It is stationary like a wall or a moat, while Koltai is like a shield, or armor that one wears and takes with them.

It would be appropriate to create several magical items using Yet-kai and place around any property you would wish to protect.

Lorash

Lorash is for improving and strengthening one's Will. Thus it is good to use while working on one's willpower or to focus one's force of will. This would be a good symbol for several different areas including overcoming bad habits or even increasing one's magical will, or when working on any sort of self discipline.

Both Yet-kai and Lorash had come to me sort of out of the blue. While doodling I felt compelled to draw the symbols. At the time I only received the names, but not what they did. So I started having folks experiment to see what they got. I, of course, got lots of conflicting answers, so I finally broke down and asked what they did. I still kept using them for testing students.

Gar-Lon

Gar-Lon is for trapping and holding spirits. The history of this symbol is rather interesting. A young lady I know had attracted the attention of what can be described as a negative spirit. I call it a negative spirit, or entity, because it did not like the use of Koltai or Grishtor (which is holy energy). This thing had latched on to her and was causing her grief. When I did a working on the young lady with Koltai and Grishtor, she almost immediately felt pain and wanted me to stop. I interpreted this to mean that the negative entity did not like the holy energy and was causing her pain so that I would stop. I and another Rún Valdr person did what we could to pull it out of the young woman. As stated before, I would have to question anyone who reacted negatively to Grishtor as this is purely holy energy.

I then thought that it would have been really nice to have had a symbol to trap the spirit and then fill it with Grishtor, maybe Thurisaz so that once the spirit was trapped inside it could be thoroughly destroyed by the combination of Grishtor and Thurisaz. Or maybe use Han-so instead of Thurisaz so that it could be transformed by the holiness of Grishtor into something more positive.

One could also create a magical object out of a jar with a lid that could be fastened to create a more permanent spirit trap. Using the information from the magical object chapter this would be fairly easy to make. I would caution the reader to be careful with this symbol as one would not want to trap a beneficial spirit, or even that of a departed loved one who happened to be still hanging around for whatever reason. One should be very sure that any spirit trapped using this symbol is deserving of it. Feedback from a student experimenting with this symbol that hitting the dot in the center can release whatever is trapped in it.

This is a neat symbol to use for testing as it is the one that most people get right. Just looking at the symbol draws one's eyes towards the dot in the middle and it's hard to look away. When I look at it I can feel my attention and mind being drawn inwards. Because of this almost instinctual reaction just looking at the plain symbol I would say that this is one of the more powerful symbols that I've collected. So use it with care.

Rún Valdr Certificates

Personally I have never really felt the need to make Rún Valdr certificates. I realize that this is a big deal with the Reiki crowd, but it not something I really think is necessary for this system. Not that I'm forbidding anyone to create Rún Valdr certificates or anything, but you probably won't get one from me unless you ask for it specifically and then I'll probably grumble about it. Either way I will leave it up to you if you want to bother with certificates.

Un-Attuning

I once did a distance attunement to a person in India. Afterwards they wrote to me telling me that Rún Valdr is not the same as Reiki and demanded that I un-attune them. Apparently the Rún Valdr energy was not meshing well with them. I remember thinking how am I supposed to un-attune someone? That's kind of like becoming a virgin again, or unchopping down a tree. It didn't seem possible to me. But the person sounded really desperate, so I figured I should do something.

I went to Odin and explained the situation and asked if there was some way to un-attune someone. He looked at me and then gave me a symbol and instructions.

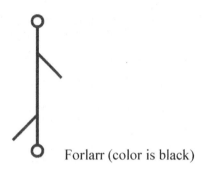

Forlarr (color is black)

During the un-attunement, the bottom circle is at the second chakra while the top circle is just above the person's head.

Picture all the symbols moving from the second chakra to the top circle and then dissipating upward. Once all the symbols have been removed in this way use Lugar to shut down the connection to the Rún Valdr energy. Say:

"By the Power and authority of Odin and Freyja, let this person be un-attuned (or de-attuned if you want to use that word) to the energies of Rún Valdr. Let this gift be taken back, now and forever more." I then thought to seal this with the Reiki Power symbol as I had been taught to seal Reiki attunements with this symbol.

Looking back I wonder if Odin wasn't just having fun with me. After the un-attunement I got an e-mail from the person in India saying that it hadn't worked and that they were still attuned to Rún Valdr and I needed to do something. I ended up telling him to meditate on Shai Nal and that it would even out the energy and after than just to not use the system and like an atrophied muscle would, over time, not work.

The advice seemed to have worked as they eventually wrote that things were better. Or maybe the un (or de) -attuning took some time to work. Most likely the attunement process just normally worked its course and settled down. Still this is probably a good time to stress again that Rún Valdr is not Reiki. It shares some qualities, but the energy source is different. Do not think that the two systems are interchangeable or even compatible.

It is important that your future students are not confused on this issue and see Rún Valdr as just some other flavor of Reiki. I also wonder if the Norse cultural properties limit the usefulness of the system to folks of completely different cultures. A devout Japanese Buddhist may have issues with the wild Norse energies, for example.

I'm sharing the un- or de-attuning symbol and process, not because I think it works, but to give you, the student, as much information as possible related to Rún Valdr.

Final Thoughts on Attunements

This covers performing Rún Valdr attunements. I will say again that giving an attunement is simply one of the most magical and cool things you can do. I always feel really good after giving attunements and it is always an honor to pass on my system to others. It is my goal to have Rún Valdr spread among the inhabitants of Earth so that when we do eventually meet other species out in space we will be known as a powerful race of healers and miracle workers.

So get out there, do some attunements and spread the word of Odin and Freyja!

Chapter Six
Rún Valdr Magic

In a previous chapter we learned about the standard Rún Valdr working. Beyond the formal Rún Valdr working already covered, readers/student may want to find flexible ways to perform magic while still using the Rún Valdr system. One way is by creating magical objects, which will be covered in the next chapter. Sometimes the formal working is not the right approach, but a need for a systemic magical approach is still needed.

First let us define what "magic" means. Aleister Crowley's definition seems to be popular and states that magic (or magick) is "the Science and Art of causing Change to occur in conformity with Will." This is a good definition and many authors of magic use it. This then leads to discussions of the Will, what it is and how to apply it towards magic. Essentially the Will is the force behind your magic. It is the vehicle for the magical act. Crowley liked to define the Will as an aspect of one's Higher Self and all acts of magic should be used to a greater understanding of this Higher Self. Crowley, of course, used magic for plenty of practical goals, so don't be concerned with that.

I asked Odin and Freyja about a magical system to use with Rún Valdr. Odin's definition of magic is "Interfacing with the forces of Nature and/or the mechanisms of the Universe to manifest a desire or goal into the realm of Midgard, or elsewhere." This definition places less importance on the individual Will, but instead focus on working with the existing meta-systems to get the work done. One thing that Odin and Freyja mentioned was the importance of gaining authority in order to make the change. In this case authority is having the right or dominion over something. Thus, to work magic you would need to gain authority, even if it's temporary, over something in order to make the changes you need. The term authority is incorporated into the name Rún Valdr, which means rune power, or authority.

To use an example, if I wanted plumbing done in my house I could call a plumber. The plumber has the proper training and has authority over plumbing issues and I would, in this case, be borrowing the plumber's authority temporarily (Which is kind of like Theurgy). I could learn to do plumbing myself and thus gain my own authority (Thaumaturgy). However, if I wanted to make changes to plumbing techniques for all of the United States of America, or to change the type of materials used, I would need to be able to influence either a large plumbing union or the plumbing trade commission (or some similar organization) for the country. Otherwise a single individual could not hope to change how every plumber in the country does things. This is the challenge of working magic. To gain the correct amount of authority so that the changes you make actually are taken seriously.

Traditional magic perhaps relies on the Neo-Theosophical idea that reality is made up of several planes of existence, each eventually leading to manifestation in the physical plane. This is the foundation of creative visualization and a majority of modern magic. Even the Kabbalah starts with Kether (nothingness or totality of everything) moving down the Tree of Life until you come to the physical world, thus creating a map of manifestation or creation. The idea is that anything physical first existed in the causal plane, then the mental plane, then the astral plane, to finally it is manifested in the physical (the number of planes and how they are named seems to vary depending on what source you use). However that idea needs enough energy to carry it through the manifestation process. In a way, having enough energy to carry through to the next lower plane is a form of authority. The idea needs to be potent enough to manifest.

Common day dreams are the stuff of the mental and astral planes. However, these idle thoughts have little energy to actually manifest. With creative visualization or other magical practices where you consistently and repetitively visualize your goal, you are empowering your thoughts so that they have weight, gravity, density (authority), what have you, to actually be manifested. You could say that there is a current towards manifestation so that any thought with enough energy will eventually manifest. This creates a sort of consensual reality where a lot of people expecting something will get it, as all that energy is being focused on one thing. It also explains why ideas before their time fail.

Look at e-readers. Sony had electronic book readers long before Amazon came out with the Kindle. However the time was ripe when the Kindle hit the market and the whole idea took off to the point where Amazon says they sell more electronic books than physical ones and large book stores like Borders closed because they could not adapt to the new electronic market.

What does this have to do with Rún Valdr? Odin stated that these different levels of reality are more interconnected than I had thought. For example, I could think about a sculpture that I may want to create. I could see it in my mind, plan it out, and go through the motions of sculpting it. This would follow the traditional idea that things manifest from the mental plane down. However, Odin said that one could just start slapping clay together and see what kind of sculpture you get. You could create a wonderful sculpture without thinking about it first. So the linear descent of idea into physical manifestation is not always that linear.

To create change magically sometimes half the battle is making sure you are not swimming against the tide. You could be an excellent swimmer, but won't make much headway if the tide is against you. Knowing the direction of the tide first is a great benefit. If you could change the tide, that would give you the greatest advantage. In my mind, gaining the proper authority over something can allow you to change the tide. The rest after that is easy.

Well if we look at orlog, or the Norse idea of fate, we can see the ancient Norse equivalent of a consensual reality. Orlog is fate in that it is the momentum of everyone's past actions upon the moment, this weight and momentum is more or less headed in a certain way. In other words, it has force and a vector. While you can change orlog, it is tough because it has all that weight behind it. I look at orlog as everyone's wills trying to find manifestation. The world you see around you is the result of this combined effort. It is like a tide of human will. Orlog can be changed, even drastically, however, you need the proper authority in order to make those changes. And because everyone is trying to manifest things you may need a greater authority to fight against the chaos.

Instead of a system where manifestation flows from the causal plane to the mental plane, to the astral plane, to the physical plane, Odin and Freyja talked about how the other realms, Upper and Under act as places where authority is derived. The Gods can do a lot, however there are a lot of Gods and they have their own consensual reality to deal with. There are many Gods of the air who deal with weather, but They won't interfere with each other, so they limit what they can or will do directly.

So human magicians need to find authority to do their work. There are three ways to gain authority.

1. Ask for it.

2. Work for it, gaining skills, put energy into it.

3. Gain enough understanding/sympathy/resonance with an area to gain authority.

Asking for authority would come from the Gods and may be temporary, at least as long as the magical work you are doing needs to last. Of course the mere act of asking some other being to do the work is borrowing their authority in the matter, or get them to do the work. Whether you are praying for a specific result or directly asking for help with your magic from a Deity it would all fit under asking for authority. This is also what I consider to be Theurgy. Getting the Gods to do the work for you.

Most shamanic work also deals with meeting various entities to gain their help to do things, thus sharing in that being's authority. If you want to change the weather, make friends with Gods or other entities that are responsible for weather change and ask/gain authority to do the same. Summoning demons/entities such as from the Goetia would also count as borrowing authority.

The second way would, perhaps, be more applicable to mundane activities. If I want to be a plumber, I need to go to school for plumbing, learn the trade, become an apprentice, etc. Or if I want to be a great athlete, I would need to practice every day, study everything about my chosen sport, etc. However, creative visualization uses the same techniques. By constantly imagining the goal as already manifested you are empowering that image with energy so that it will eventually manifest. While a lot of magic is fire and forget, and actually demands that you forget about the working after it's done, creative visualization demands a lot of work and focus on the goal. I would also place psychic phenomenon in this category. Psychic abilities are skills and need work to improve and expand.

The third type of merging or gaining resonance is similar to the second method, but could possibly take longer. You are essentially attuning yourself to area of influence so much that you are seen as a key part of that area so that when you make changes it is accepted naturally. Nikola Tesla, the inventor of AC electricity dealt with resonance later in his life and there are stories of his experiments shaking the building he was living in. He reportedly said that if he could find the resonance of the planet he could crack it open. Thus resonance can be a tool to make changes or to gain authority.

This is the method used mostly be ceremonial magicians who vibrate various names of God and enflame themselves with prayer in order to gain enough of God's authority to do what they want. Traditional magical work with spirits, sometimes called Spirit Arte is famous for this kind of authority. By enflaming themselves with prayer the magician would gain the necessary authority of God (by associating themselves with Gods might) to command the spirits, demons, or angels to do whatever the magician required. Technically this would be a hybrid of the first and third ways. You are gaining resonance in order to gain help of others and thus make use of their authority to get what you want.

Going back to the weather analogy, if you want to change the weather you could spend time trying to become one with the sky and all the things in it. By identifying with the sky completely you become one with it, or gain resonance with it. Thus when you want to change the weather you merely plug in your wish and the sky accepts the change because it has come to accept you as being a part of it. I came up with an elemental magical model based on this. You would fill yourself with one of the four classic elements (earth, fire, air or water) and use that energy to accomplish a goal. The idea was that you were not only filled with it, but you were in contact with the infinite element allowing it to manifest within you. You became infinite earth, or fire, etc.

Looking back, I also cured myself of my migraines by a similar method. I would visualize myself as being filled with pink light, the color of bubble gum or rose quartz. This would lessen the severity of the migraine and over time would prevent them, and finally I stopped getting them altogether.

I suppose that creative visualization would overlap with this as well. You are spending so much time attuning with the final result that you gain authority to manifest it.

On a quicker note, a lot of kitchen magic, or natural magic makes use of this kind of authority. This springs from magical laws of sympathy. Putting energy into a green candle, which represents wealth will then bring wealth when lit. I will go more into how the various magical laws are connected to the idea of authority and resonance a bit later.

Once you have your magical authority sorted out the magical work is then broken down into four steps.

1. Asking/gaining authority.

2. Merging or gaining resonance with area to change

3. Make the changes

4. Finishing up.

In step one you would ask for authority for the magical working. Or you would have gained the authority in some way. If doing a more complete or full ritual you could make offerings to whatever Deity you are getting help from at this point.

In step two you would spend time attuning yourself to the area that you are trying to change. This part is separate from the third method of gaining authority in that instead of trying to gain authority you are trying to create resonance to make the change you want. You need to become the thing you are trying to change.

Step three is the meat and potatoes of the working. Since you have made a connection in step two you should reach out and feel/see the changes you are making. Kind of like sculpting. Feel the change happening and know that it is changing reality.

Step four is equally as important. You need to finish correctly or your efforts could be in vain. If sticking with Rún Valdr, you would obviously use the sealing symbol, Tunai. I would also recommend stating out loud a definitive statement such as, "By my authority over X, let this be so!", or "By my authority, I set these changes to be made manifest."

For specific techniques, here are some ideas that can be applied to Rún Valdr.

For gaining authority, you could use a Deity symbol within you and allow the energy to fill you to overflowing. Deity symbols will be dealt with later in chapter eight, but is essentially a symbol that represents the presence of a Deity. You can also gain symbols for things like the Universe, or other powers.

There is a symbol, which I have included in chapter eight that can be used for gaining resonance. It would be used much the same way as Reloxon, where you are in one end and the target is in the other.

These principles can be incorporated when doing more standard Rún Valdr workings.

Thoughts on Seidh Work

I had another conversation with Freyja and Odin about seidh work and trance journey work in general. Seidh work deals with traveling to the other worlds and making contact with various spirits for a variety of purposes. This type of work is the heart and soul of shamanic work of all kinds. Seidh can be seen as Norse shamanism to a great extent. To be fair, there is some argument as to whether Seidh really dealt with journey work, but for the sake of this section we will include any shamanic and/or trance journey work as falling under the auspices of Seidh.

Either you are trying to gain knowledge, or you are trying to get a spirit to do something for you. Typically the knowledge aspect involves you traveling to a specific location; Helheim, Asgard, or some other place and asking questions of spirits or Deities, and is how I got the information for Rún Valdr from Odin and Freyja. I am also including in seidh work, contacting specific spirits to do magical work for you.

This is similar to grimoiric magic that may be familiar to those with some training in ceremonial magic. This is the kind of magic you see in grimoires such as the Lesser Key of Solomon (also known as the Goetia), or the Greater Key of Solomon, that have great list of demons and angels, each with a description of the spirit, what they do and also what their sigil is. I'm sure ancient seidh workers had friendly spirits that would help them by performing tasks. But from lore this idea is not supported very well.

Traditionally, at least from a Norse lore perspective, a seidh worker would travel to Helheim to speak with the spirits of the dead for information (as seen in the Voluspa), or would attract spirits to the seidh worker where questions would be asked (as used by the seidh woman described in Eirik's Saga). There are also stories of sorcerers using seidh to harm others which in one story involved them sitting on the victim's roof chanting songs that ended up killing a boy who was lured out, also by the songs. These techniques (hopefully not the killing parts) can be adapted to a modern scenario, and also can be simplified to some extent by using tools from Rún Valdr.

You are not limited to just traveling to Helheim. You could go to Asgard or Vanaheim to talk with the Deities there. You could go to both Alfheims to gain knowledge of nature and crafting. You could go to Muspelheim, the land of fire, and Niflheim, the land of ice where the two basic forces that created the universe come from. You can even make offerings to Yggdrasil to gain the World Tree as an ally. This is basically what Odin did when He won knowledge of the runes. His offering to Yggdrasil was Himself and, in this case, Odin was granted resonance with Yggdrasil where the knowledge of the runes flowed out and into Him. Yggdrasil, being in contact with all the worlds, kind of acts as a repository for wisdom, like the akashic records.

I asked about gaining authority over the spirits involved. Odin stated that having Himself and Freyja as Patrons leaves a mark that grants authority, or a tendency for certain kinds of spirits to be more open or friendly with those having such a patronage. Thus spirits associated with things that Odin and Freyja have authority over; war, abundance, poetry, battle, wisdom, magic (galdr and seidh), sex, as well as raven, wolf, boar and falcon spirits would be friendlier towards you. Basically, any Deity that acts as a Patron for a human, will leave this mark that helps smooth the way for the human. Even marks from old Patrons that may not actively be around anymore will still be valid.

Freyja said, "Oh you and your 'authority," in a rather dismissive fashion. She wasn't very impressed with having authority and her chastisement was directed at Odin as well as to myself. Freyja explained that authority was only important with galdr where you are trying to directly change things. With spirit, or seidh work, less emphasis is placed on authority and more on reciprocity and forging alliances with spirits. It is the spirit who does the work, and they already have the authority. You are just trying to get them to cooperate. This is like my plumbing analogy above where you are borrowing the authority of the plumber by getting them to do the work for you. However, you are not seeking to have authority over the spirit, instead you are building a working relationship with that spirit.

You gain cooperation by making offerings to the spirits. When making contact with specific spirits who will be doing magical work for you, this amounts to two different things. Making offerings, either physical or energetic and also making a very specific kind of physical offering. Normally in spirit arte, much is made of having a sigil of the spirit to aid in the calling of them to you. This sigil or symbol can be carved into a physical substance (wood, metal, etc). This kind of offering is attractive to spirits as it gives them a greater tie to the physical world. The engraving of the sigil is usually done after the spirit has agreed to work with you. They may require other offerings for the actual magical work.

Regarding offerings, alcohol or food make good offerings, as does incense. When dealing with spirits of the dead, however, the food should not have any salt in it. Spirits of the dead, according to Martin Coleman in his book *Communing With The Spirits*, are unable to absorb energy from food that contains salt. It is a good idea to ask the spirit, once you have contacted it, what kind of offering they would like in exchange for their work. Don't be afraid to negotiate with the spirit if it asks for something inappropriate. For example if an abundance spirit asks for a hand full of solid gold coins, feel free to say no, and seek an offering that you could actually make.

You can also offer your own energy. I was told that you could draw energy from your body, this is kind of like the energy used when exercising or while doing physical excursion. I see it as a blue ball of energy that I draw from by chest and then hand to the spirit. This is a general currency type of thing that can be given to any spirit as an offering when negotiating with them. I was told that under no circumstance should this be an offering of parts of your soul. You are basically taking energy from the physical body only. Freyja also mentioned, in regards to offerings, that the energy from orgasms is a particularly good offering to make and is usually very well received.

Getting back to the idea of having a sigil of the spirit to be engraved, there are techniques to create the sigil from the name of the spirit where letters are carefully arranged in a certain pattern and you spell out the name by moving from one letter to the next. The picture you end up with is the sigil. However I like the idea of asking the spirit for the symbol better. It is basically what I did with Odin and Freyja to get the symbols used in Rún Valdr. I would ask them for a symbol that would do X and they gave it to me. Basically after contacting a spirit and it agreeing to work with you, you would ask it for a symbol representing its presence which you can then get engraved on some object. This symbol will also act to make contact with the spirit for any future work that might be done.

Freyja also talked about coming up with a sigil to represent yourself and offering this to the spirit as well. This helps create a closer relationship between you and the spirit. To be honest I had never heard of doing this before but it makes sense from a reciprocity/partnership point of view. But I would urge caution. You would be giving that spirit means of contacting you directly, so make sure the spirit or entity you give this symbol to is trustworthy.

When dealing with offerings for spirits where you are visiting a specific place and asking whatever spirits happen to be there for information, more general offerings would be in order. Using Reloxoné to fill an area with energy comes in handy. Or before your travel you could have made a general offering of alcohol or food to the spirits. If you are so inclined you could also use Reloxoné on yourself and then project the energy to the spirit. Dorva is a great symbol for sending energy.

There are modern groups today that do seidh work. Two of these are Diana Paxson's group and Katie Gerrard's group. Diana Paxson has written *Taking Up The Runes* and *Trance-Portation*. *Taking Up The Runes* is highly recommended for the beginner learning about the runes. *Trance-Portation* is also for beginners in trance journey work and is also highly recommended. Katie Gerrard's books, *Odin's Gateways* is about using the runes for magic and divination and *Seidhr: The Gate is Open*_deals with Seidh work specifically and has good techniques. For those with interest in seidh and trance work I would highly recommend *Trance-portation* and *Seidhr*.

A key point that Gerrard makes is raising energy for the spirits to use during the seidh working. Her group uses ecstatic dance, which seems odd to me. With Rún Valdr, you already have tools to easily dump a lot of energy into any area. Simply use Reloxoné to start a conduit of energy. I would recommend this be done, with one end around the energy source and the other end around your whole working area.

A second key point is the use of songs, called vardlokkurs to attract the spirits. Freyja said that this is more important than providing energy, as not a lot of energy is needed to attract spirits, especially since you will be giving offerings to them anyway elsewhere in the rite. The vardlokkurs attract spirits, calling to them.

Freyja endorsed Gerrard's methods, although said that a substitution for ecstatic dance can be made to provide the energy needed. Again, using Reloxoné to flood the area with energy for the spirits' use is an easy way to accomplish this.

One surprising thing came from Odin. He said that the runes are spirits and could be treated with in the same way as other spirits. To be honest, I'm not sure how to take this information. If the runes are spirits then they seem to be odd spirits. Runes, at least for me, have always seemed fairly mechanical patterns of energy. They each had its function, even though each rune was rather complex and possessed multiple levels of meaning and purpose. But they never seemed to me as being alive.

Even in the sagas, runes are used in a mechanical function. Plug in runes A, B, and C, and get result X, Y, and Z. This mechanical function made them perfect for Rún Valdr. But now they have this whole other dimension to them that I never suspected. I wonder if making offerings to Fehu could be used to increase your prosperity, or Wunjo to increase your joy.

With this new idea, you could do a formal spirit summoning for any of the runes, make your offerings and ask for help with your work. Or just make offerings as part of your regular devotional work. I supposed when dealing with runes as spirits or other abstract things you can ask for them to take human shape to make it easier for you to interact with them.

It does bring up other possibilities, such as working with the spirit of Yggdrasil itself, or of the Universe. Or other seemingly abstract ideas like Love. I have made a good deal of progress contacting Yggdrasil. I find when dealing with non-human entities, such as Yggdrasil, or rather abstract things like the Universe, it helps if you ask for the entity to create a human shape that you can interact with.

I would like to look at the basic formulas for the different types of spirit work and then go into more details of the actual practice and techniques to be used as well as tips I received from Odin and Freya.

The basic formula for the information gathering seidh work is either go into a trance and journey to a location where spirit are, usually Helheim. Once there, questioners ask questions of the seer and she/he gets the answers and responds to the person. Or you attract the spirits to you and listen to their answers in response to the questions from the audience. I would make offerings before the trance work. Or you could make offerings of your own energy when you meet with the spirits, use Reloxoné, etc. You could also travel to where a spirit lived and bargain for work to be done as well.

The traditional formula for spirit magic is to summon a spirit to you, usually inside a magical circle, where you bargain/threaten the spirit into doing your bidding. This method actually involved a lot of attempts to gain authority over the spirit to force it to do what you want. In ADF, attempts have been made to use the ADF core order of ritual and the model of reciprocity to make contact with spirits in a more friendly and hospitable way. This method works very well and follows Freyja's model of cooperation and relationship. I myself have done a ritual at a festival to summon spirits of the Goddess Sif to find those willing to act as magical allies. Overall the ritual was a great success and a number of spirits were contacted.

Regarding specific techniques for trance work, Freyja mentioned that triggers are important. By triggers, I mean actions that you repeat every time you go into trance that end up acting like triggers to make it easier to enter and exit trance. Neuro-Linguistic Programming would call these "anchors." Diana Paxson talks about this in *Trance-portation* as well. Triggers are very important, for the practitioner as well as the audience. In the saga of Eirik when the seidh woman showed up. She is described in great detail as to what she is wearing. I would say that her outfit was a trigger for the audience to help put them into a receptive state so as to accept the things she would be telling them during the rite.

One important part of a seidh worker in the ancient Norse world was the high seat. This was literally a chair that sat a lot higher than normal. Think of a lifeguard chair. Being up high was important in general for seidh work, which explains why the sorcerers, discussed earlier, needed to be on the victim's roof. Getting back to the seidh woman in Eirik's saga, again, this was a trigger for the practitioner to get her in the proper mind set and also told the audience to expect otherworldly wisdom. Whether or not you want to do this for your own practice is up to you; but it is good to look at the types of triggers that were important to the ancients.

The saga goes on to describe the ritual meal the seer has, the need for the proper songs, etc. All of these were known to both the seer and the audience, and all the different parts would draw both parties deeper and deeper into the whole experience.

You need to establish your own triggers for regular trance work. Freyja suggested that when you are starting your trance, you count to ten. On each count, you see yourself moving away from your body and into the other world. On the count of ten you visualize yourself surrounded and filled by a magical fire that transports you to a location in the other world. On the return, count to ten again, but this time take a step backwards towards your body.

An inner temple (or inner hall as I like to call it) is an important thing to have, and will be a vital tool, as it becomes a staging area where you always start your trance journeys from. I would recommend that, if you are new to trance journey work, you start here. Even if you are experienced and do not have an inner hall I would encourage you to make one. Think of this space as a metaphorical front porch, a place that acts as a liaison between your mind and the other objective inner worlds that exist all around us. Any time you do a trance journey, you will start from this inner temple. When you first start making your inner hall you will be basically creating a space in your mind. It will be very subjective at first, but as you put energy into it, it will take on a life of its own. You can also use the symbol Gord (discussed later in the experimental symbols section) to help manifest it into reality.

Your inner hall can look like anything. An elaborate temple, a pyramid, a quiet grove of trees in a forest, a high plateau on some other planet, anything you like. Just be aware of what this space is and what it's for. It should have doors or doorways, or some sort of gate leading into the inner realms. As you progress you may find new doors appearing spontaneously in your inner temple.

For my trance work, I also have created a bracelet to help with trance induction. This is basically an inexpensive cloth bracelet that is adjustable that I bought from the Oriental Trading Company. I used this for the Sif spirit ritual where I handed them out to people to use during the ritual. I attuned them all with all the symbols having to do with astral projection, meditation, and protection. Not only is the energy the bracelet putting out designed to help with trance journeys, but by putting it on every time I go into trance it acts as a trigger.

Having guides can be a great benefit when on a trance journey. Shamans all over the world have guides to help them travel the inner worlds. Guides can help smooth the way when you travel or warn you of trouble. I would suggest asking your Deities for a guide and calling on them whenever you leave your inner hall.

Summoning spirits to do work for you is a traditional ceremonial magical idea and has an old and rich history. This kind of magic was very popular in the Middle Ages to the Renaissance periods. Above I mentioned using the ADF core order of ritual in context of making contact with spirits willing to work with me magically. This is actually quite different from the traditional way of dealing with spirits. However, since I am a member of ADF, the newer model fits how I see the world and have come to interact with the Kindred in general. I'll go over what I did here.

I first came across this process at an ADF Festival. Ian Corrigan did a ritual to the Goddess Brigit in order to gain working spirits to help with magic. He looked at Brigit and the areas She had authority over, namely Smithing, Poetry, and Healing. These then became her Powers, or Queens, each being represented by a spirit, sort of like a vice-president in a corporation in charge of a particular department. Under each Power is a host of smaller spirits whose job is to do the real work. It is these working spirits that the magician wants to make contact with.

During the ritual we, the participants, made contact with a wide variety of spirits who worked for one of the three Powers of Brigit. Key in this contact was their name, what they did and what they wanted as an offering for their services. I was fascinated by this process and thought that I could do the same thing for a Norse Deity. Ian chose Brigit because She has no war-like aspects and could be considered safe when doing a public festival ritual. By the same token I chose Sif to work with for the same reason.

Having chosen Sif, I did some trance work to get Her permission for this working. She was agreeable and said She had five such Powers. Later She said to call them her Chieftains. I looked at the Troth Book, *Our Troth, volume 1, History and Lore* for more information on Sif, particularly to learn what She had authority over. I read the part about Sif and took notes, writing down each aspect I came across. When I was done and counted them up, I indeed had five. These are Beauty, Abundance, Kinship (particularly through wedlock), Prophesy, and Protection. These basically became their names and I eventually came up with Old Norse equivalent: Friðr, Gnött, Frændi, Spá, and Hlif, respectively.

The next step was to meet with each of the Chieftains and gain their permission for the working I had planned. After more trance journeys, I met them and gained their permission, also learning what each wanted for an offering. This was the following: locks of hair for Friðr, coins for Gnött (denomination was not that important, but had to be real currency), bread (especially homemade) for Frændi, mead for Spá, and rowan wood (touched to the tongue before offering) for Hlif.

After this I had to plan out the ritual. This would follow a full core order of ritual for ADF (Ár nDraíocht Féin). The ritual is based on reciprocity in that offerings are made and then blessings are given in return from the Kindred (Ancestors, Nature Spirits, and the Gods)

Rituals usually start out with some offering to the Outdwellers, those beings who are antagonistic to our Gods and to humans. In a Norse perspective this would be the Jotuns, or Giants. The offerings are made so that they will leave you in peace. Then offerings are made to the Earth Mother, and the spirits of bardic inspiration. Then the Portals are opened. This is a key point in ADF rituals in that the Well, the Fire, and the Tree become portals that reach to the other worlds so that the interaction between these realms and Midgard are strengthened. A gatekeeper Deity is often used to help open these Gates and to watch over them. Then offerings are made to the three Kindred and finally to the Deity of the Occasion, the Deity that is the focus of the ritual. After all the offerings have been made an omen is taken to determine if the offerings have been accepted or what blessings we can expect in return. This is the part of the ritual where actual dialogue (albeit indirect) can be gained between those present and the Kindred. If the offerings have been accepted then the return blessings are prepared, blessed and passed out to the participants. Then we thank everyone involved in reverse order, including closing the Gates.

I find it to be a very powerful devotional rite and it worked well when used in the working with Sif and Her spirits. I had bought a prodigious amount of alcohol for offerings and made the magical bracelets for everyone to use.

For the ritual I made offerings to the Jotuns for the Outdwellers, Jorð for the Earth Mother, Bragi for bardic inspiration, used Thor as the Gatekeeper, and made offerings to the Kindred to gain Their help in protection for the rite. Sif got a couple of offerings and each of the Chieftains as well. The working spirits got a bottle of single malt scotch. I also made sure to use vardlokkur to attract the spirits.

This ritual required the participants to go into a trance journey state to interact with the spirits summoned and this was a tricky part. But in steps I led them further and further along the path so I feel that when the time came for the actual trance work they were prepared.

After all the offerings were made, the vardlokkurs sung, the participants were in trance journey mode, I asked the spirits assembled to only stay if they were willing to work with us in safety and frith. I asked this three times and there were spirits that left. Those that remained were invited to interact with the participants.

Contact was made with sixteen spirits from all the Chieftains except Friðr. In this case, I asked the participants to ask for their name, what they did, what offering they wanted and what their symbol was.

If you are interested in doing this with your own Deity, and do not want to bother with a big festival ritual, I recommend the following suggestions. First do trance journey work to visit your Deity and see if They are willing to help you in this fashion. After doing research to find out exactly what Their Chieftains will be, have your Deity make the appropriate introductions, again as part of trance journey work. Then you can work with each Chieftain asking for introductions to individual spirits, either depending on what you want or up to the whim of the Chieftain. When talking with the individual spirit, get their name, what they do, and what they want in return for their work. If you can, get their symbol.

The next step after identifying a spirit you want to work with is to come up with some ritual to actually work with them. I decided that a modified ADF core order of ritual would work. You would leave out a lot, sticking with the very basics. It would require trance journey work in the middle of it, so having an inner temple would be crucial. Having a spirit manifest physically in the physical world is not very realistic, despite the lore. However, summoning them to your inner hall solves this problem. Either that or you do lots of work to see and hear spirits from the physical, waking world. I find using an inner temple and a trance journey work to be the easiest solution.

The outline is based on a Norse cultural perspective, but it can be modified to fit your own needs.

Outdwellers: The mighty Jotunkind
Earth mother: Jorð
Open Portals/Gatekeeper: Whomever you deem appropriate.
Deity offering. Make offering and ask for aid and authority in magical working.

Chieftain in question offering. Make offering and ask for aid and authority in magical working

Worker spirit in question offering. Make offering that they prefer, asking that they appear when summoned.

Trance induction to inner temple (this section will be done during a trance journey in a ritual area you create in your inner hall)

> Summoning of spirit (use of symbol as a focus, calling by the authority of Deity and the specific Chieftain)
>
> Interaction with spirit (asking for task to be done, settling on final price, establishing time frame, etc.)
>
> License to depart and thanks to the worker spirit
>
> Come out of trance to finish rite.

Thanking the specific spirit

Thanking Chieftain

Thanking Deity

Thanking Gatekeeper/closing gates

Thanking Earth mother

Thanking Outdwellers

End of rite.

Again, the real key is the trance journey work with the other parts of the ritual acting as a framework for the trance work and as a place to make physical offerings to prepare for the meeting and conversation with the spirit.

Your inner hall should have an appropriate place set up, complete with a space for the spirit to arrive and depart. Depending on your needs, this summoning place may be in a separate area from your normal space.

After the spirit has done the work you have requested you can do another ritual to thank it and to perhaps make more offerings. This follow up is important as it helps to further establish and to grow your relationship with the spirit you are working with.

Ethical Considerations When Doing Magic

If you want something to eat, you may get in your car and drive to a grocery store or a restaurant. We all do what we can to influence the world in ways that we want, whether to gain what we want or to avoid things we don't want. We can use skills to dig a hole, build a house, fix a car, create a landscape painting, do the dishes, or get a job. Magic is a tool, much like any other skill you possess. Is there any difference ethically whether you use magic to do something or use mundane means? My short answer is no.

When reading books on the occult in my youth, they spoke a great deal of not using magic to harm others or to allow harm to come to others from the result of doing magic. One book on teleportation even went to far as to say that after you got to your destination you should not disturb anything, even picking up a rock, as you didn't have the right to change anything. This seems needlessly and overly liberal. I mean if I were to walk to the same location and pick up a rock to take home no one would think twice about it. But because I'm using "magic", i.e. teleportation, suddenly I don't have the right to impose my will on a rock? I'm not buying it. We impose our will on the physical world on a daily basis. From driving to work to eating food to trying to convince your boss to extend the deadline of your project. As physical beings, we have no choice but to impose our will upon the world. There are, however, lots of rules, like not stealing, or killing others. Traffic lights need to be obeyed, etc. Same with magic.

Like I said, magic is a tool much like any other skill or tool you possess. Why not use it to get what you need or want? I could argue that those who are inherently successful are subconsciously using principles of magic to get what they want. In the above example about driving to the grocery store in a car to get food. Your car is a valuable tool. It can take you places. It can also be used to hit people in an attempt to harm them. Does this make a motor vehicle intrinsically bad because it can be used to harm? I would argue no, just like a kitchen knife that one might use to chop up vegetables for a soup can also be used to stab someone. Neither the car nor the knife, or even a gun by itself, is intrinsically evil or harmful. They are just tools. Magic is the same and I don't really make a distinction between using magic and any other tool. I could use magic to heal someone with an infection, or just give the person some anti-biotics. I could use magic to harm someone or I could walk up and hit them with a baseball bat. The tool I use makes no difference, only the result I create.

Instead, how tools are used determines if the will you are imposing on the world is good or bad. There are ethical considerations in how you use the available tools. Knowledge and a wide variety of tools allow you to do more. As Odin teaches, knowledge is power and power is the ability to do work. The more you know, the more you can do. Magic is simply more tools we can use to create an environment we want.

I'm firmly in the camp that feels the Gods don't do too much in the physical world. If They do, They would interfere too much with our free will. This explains why bad things happen even though the Gods love us. Humans have the capability to do both good and evil. The choice is ours. It is up to us to learn to live together. The Gods can guide us, teach us and love us, but They can't live our lives for us, just like parents can't, ultimately, live the lives of their children.

This leaves us with the freedom to do as we please (within reason) because the Gods don't have some plan that They are forcing us to live by. Christians are big on saying that God has a plan for us and expects Him to pretty much run their lives for them. Then they get upset when they read about some child being killed by a psycho killer. The question as to why God allows evil to exist is pretty much the core of any Christian who doubts their religion. They fail to realize that any God will not intervene too much for fear of abrogating free will. I'm sure They will nudge things if they can find plausible deniability, but directly intervene? I find this increasingly hard to believe. Although I will admit that if we invite the Gods into our lives, we give permission for a certain amount of interference from Them. I tend to take the Norse view that this world is ours to shape as we see fit. The meaning of life is to live this life as fully as possible.

What does this all have to do with magic? Well even though the Gods may not (or will not) directly intervene in the mortal realm, we are born with abilities beyond the physical that can be used to get things done. I would not worry about upsetting some grand divine plan by using magic, no more than one would worry about dismantling some cosmic plan by driving faster than the speed limit dictates because you are running late.

However since magic can affect things on a large scale (weather working comes to mind) it is always good to look to see what the outcomes may be of our magical working. The concern is not so much will it succeed or not, because if you are going to bother to use magic you need to believe and accept that it will work or you shouldn't bother. However, if we push things this way, will we be screwing ourselves down the road in a way we hadn't anticipated? Being human our view is much more limited than that of the Gods. Gods can read the patterns of our actions and have a pretty good idea as to how things will turn out. Not being Gods it behooves us to try to learn how the outcome of our magical practice has in the long run. Basically we need to know if our magical working will cause any harm. If not, great. If so, then we need to know how and whether this is acceptable.

Before you condemn me as a heartless monster it should be reminded that in 2010 there were 32,885 automobile related deaths in the United States. While this is a tiny fraction of the population, it is the size of a small town. Losing a small town a year is a price we pay for the convenience of using automobiles. This seems to be an acceptable loss or drastic steps would be taken to eliminate automobile related deaths which would most likely make driving a car very problematic compared to the relative freedom we have now (even with all the rules we are to follow).

I am not condoning an attitude that we can do whatever we want and to hell with the consequences, but some harm is more acceptable than others. As humans, our bodies kill billions of bacteria every day. Is this violence good? Necessary? I would say yes. Demolition of old buildings to make way for new ones is good, unless you don't make sure all the people are out of the building first, or if you don't bother to protect the area surrounding the building and just plant the explosive willy nilly. The first step is determining how the outcome of your magical working will affect things. You should do this for major physical undertakings as well. Divination is a good way to do this.

I would of course suggest that the runes be used in this endeavor. A simple three rune reading can be done asking the question, "what will be the final outcome of my magical work to do X?" or "What will be the outcome if I use magic to do X?" As Donald Michael Kraig says in his book, <u>Modern Magick</u> when talking about doing tarot readings to determine the outcome of a magical working, "Do not ask 'Should I do such-and such?' as this puts the responsibility for your actions on the cards rather than on you. You should be seeking advice, not asking a pseudo-mommy for instructions."

I agree with this. Asking whether or not you should do something should be determined much earlier. To use an analogy, you are not asking if you should go to restaurant Y or restaurant X, you are asking the outcome if you take route Z to get to the restaurant that you have already chosen. Will there be a traffic jam? Will you be delayed due to construction? Will you get lost? Will you end up in an accident? Will you get food poisoning from the lobster?

By asking what the outcome will be if you use magic to achieve X results you are trying to get a glimpse beyond your normal limited human vision to see the broader scope of things. No one exists in a vacuum and your actions do affect others. The aim is to make sure your actions are as positive as possible.

And of course the scope of the magic comes into play here. If you are doing magic to help yourself have a positive attitude there is no need for divination as you are affecting only yourself. Most people don't do divinations to see the outcome for a shopping trip either. However, doing weather magic can have widespread negative consequences if you are not careful. Any time you mess with systems larger than just yourself you run the risk of affecting things in a negative way simply because you are not aware of all the variables. But I would caution against getting too obsessed with this or you will find yourself unable to do any magic for fear of harming a passing mosquito or dust mite. Keep things in perspective.

Getting back to the divination. I find that using a three rune reading can give a lot of detail. I normally look at the three runes together to make a story. I am usually not reading them as past, present future, but kind of like a sentence. A lot of times the runes need to be read "out of order," that is not being read from left to right, but assembled together in a way that makes the clearest story.

If the outcome is positive, then go ahead with your magic. If it is negative you might want to hold off until a better time. Or maybe you need to re-think what you are doing or the goals you had in mind.

Other ethical considerations is in getting permission to do healing for someone before you start your working as I've already discussed in Chapter Four. Or for any other work that directly affects someone else. Having someone come up to you and ask for healing is great, but what if they relate that their Great Aunt is suffering from arthritis and could use some help? If you don't have explicit permission from the recipient should you continue, even with something as benign as healing? Most people will say, yes, you need permission before doing any working. You could do a distance working, and after using Reloxon to connect you with the recipient you could talk to their Higher Self, or other part of them open to communication and explain what you want to do. Tell them (and also have the intent) that you will doing healing work and if they don't wish to receive it then the healing will be blocked. Then go ahead and do the working. Or you could just physically ask permission.

Because Rún Valdr doesn't have the same safeguards that Reiki does, you need to be aware of what you are doing, your intentions need to be clear.

Laws of Magic seen from the perspective of Resonance and Authority

One can look at the different laws of magic and apply the concepts of resonance and authority to them. This shows how important these two ideas really are.

Laws of Magic - From *The Divine Thunderbolt* by Jane Sibley, Appendix. The laws and examples are quoted straight from *The Divine Thunderbolt*. Additional comments are my own. I have rearranged the laws in order to group them appropriately by resonance, authority or both.

Those laws dealing with resonance show that one thing can affect another by being similar to it, or by resonating with it. Laws dealing with authority set rules for what can be affected and how. Laws dealing with both are a blend of resonance and authority behavior.

Resonance Laws

1. The Law of Similarity: Magic performed on (or using) one object which is similar or identical to another will affect that other object. **Resonance**

Example: A drawing or simulacrum of an axe will be as effective, magically speaking, as a genuine axe.

A clear example of how one item once it has gained resonance with another item can affect that other item. Because they are similar or identical looking they have obvious and strong resonance and each can affect the other. In the case of a picture representing an actual physical item one sees that the mere form of something is enough to grant resonance.

2. The Law of Identity: A piece of an object or organism is as effective, magically speaking, as the entire object or organism. **Resonance**

Example: A picture or symbol of the beak of a curled beak bird provides the same effect as a picture or symbol of the entire bird.

Again, a part of something gives resonance so that it can represent the whole. A part is not truly disconnected from the whole.

3. The Law of Contiguity: Any piece of a given item remains, magically speaking, part of that entire item, and retains the thaumaturgical identity of the whole. **Resonance**

Example: Each granule of powder scraped from a belemnite "thunderbolt" retains the identity and curative powers of that particular intact belemnite.

This is very similar to the Law of Identity but from the other direction. Where with the Law of Identity if you start with something that is a part of a whole such as a beak of a bird this small piece can act as if it is the whole bird. With the Law of Contiguity if you take a piece from the whole it retains the properties of the whole. Thus if start with a bird and break off the beak, or feet, those pieces would retain the qualities of the whole bird.

Both Resonance and Authority Law

1. The Law of Attraction: If a certain phenomenon or effect is desired to occur at a given location, a dramatic enactment incorporating or mimicking essential features of that desired phenomenon should attract the genuine article. **Resonance and Authority**

Example: Attracting a thunderstorm by making sparks fly, sprinkling water on the ground, firing a cannon, or beating on a drum or cooking pans; attracting wind by whistling. Everyone knows that washing one's car tends to bring a rainstorm.

This is standard resonance practices and a good example of ways to gain resonance with something. However you are going further in that you are specifically linking sprinkling of water on the ground as being equal to having the "Good Rains" fall. Otherwise sprinkling water on the ground is just normal water falling to earth with no magical connection or power behind it.

Thus you are seeking authority over the greater at the same time you are trying to achieve resonance with the greater.

2. The Law of Sympathy: A given magical effect will occur in greater format if induced in the lesser. **Resonance and Authority**

Example: Pain or disease induction may be induced in a subject by using a doll or miniature model which resembles or stands for that subject.

This is the classic voodoo doll that most are familiar with. Usually the doll has a lock of hair or nail clippings to add to the resonance. Not only that, but the lesser form grants access or authority over the greater. As above, so below and as below, so above.

3. The Law of Assimilation: The magical effect which has been produced in an item is transferred to the living being which ingests it. **Resonance and Authority**

Example: Water in which a thunderbolt core has been placed is given to a sick cow in order to cure her.

Here you see both resonance, the water in which the thunderbolt core gains resonance and thus the power of the thunderbolt core. But that power is transferred to another medium that does not have any other obvious resonance with the power object. There is not really any obvious connections between water and a thunderbolt core, but through the Law of Assimilation, the water gains authority to gain resonance with the thunderbolt core.

Authority Laws

1. The Law of Transference: A given magical effect can be transferred or sent from one object to another. **Authority**

Example: A thunderbolt core placed in the loft of a house confers its protection from one object to another.

Here you are taking the magical properties of one thing and transferring it to another. Thus you are seeking the authority to link one item with another dissimilar item in order for them to work together. Basically you are telling the magical effect what its boundaries are.

2. The Law of Relevance: One or more items or organisms which have been acted upon (or changed in some way) by another item or organism remain linked to that specific item. **Authority**

Example: The specific warriors over whom a spearshaft inscribed with a magical spell was thrown would be relevant to that specific spearshaft and its' magical spell. Other warriors, who had another enchanted spearshaft pass over them, would not be relevant to the first spell, even though the end result produced by each spell may have been the same.

A clear case of authority. Even though both spells mentioned in the example do the same thing, their targets are different and specific. One spell that targets x, y, and z, can't interfere with a spell that has already targeted a, b, and c. Even if the magical effects are essentially the same specific authority has already been established.

3. The Law of Contagion: The magical effect which has been imparted to a specific item can "infect" whatever touches it. **Authority**

Example: A cursed object will case bad luck to anyone who touches, owns, or takes possession of it, sometimes even if the cursed object is discarded or destroyed afterward.

Another case of authority. The cursed item has a great deal of authority on the target. It is granted authority over anyone who fulfills the criteria set for it regardless of lack of prior resonance.

4. The Law of Association: A magical effect is produced in an item by naming it and using it as a given, specific magical item. **Authority**

Example: Defining and using a spearhead as a thunderbolt core will cause that spearhead to display supernatural thunderbolt related effects as a result.

This is a purely authoritative driven law. By naming something as magical thing X, item Y will have the same qualities of magical thing X. In a way this is what the Wizard of Oz does with the Scarecrow, the Tinman and the Cowardly Lion in the movie. He gives a diploma to the Scarecrow thus naming him smart, and he is. He gives a "heart" to the Tinman, who suddenly gains emotions, and he gives a medal of bravery to the Lion who then becomes brave. Granted by the time of the awards, each had already proven themselves, but that final seal of approval was important.

One could also extend this out to a Law of Naming, where being able to name a thing gives one power over it. Thus it confers authority by virtue of knowledge. Knowledge is power. The more you know about something the more you can manipulate it to suit your own needs. Look at humans, we went from waiting for lightning to strike to get fire to creating nuclear furnaces.

5. The Law of Exclusion: If a given phenomenon or series of phenomena have been induced, certain other effects or phenomena cannot take place at the same time. **Authority**

Example: If one has induced a thunderstorm to come and the Good Rains fall, then a "fair weather/bright sun" spell could not work at the same time.

An important law for the physical world. You can't have to contradictory things happening at once. It cannot be both nightime and daytime at the same moment. This sets limits on effects to avoid paradoxical results.

6. The Law of Specification: If specific parameters are set, a given spell will selectively affect only those targets which fall within the specifications. If no limits are set, anyone or anything can be affected. If blurry or ambiguous parameters are set, the results could be quite unexpected. **Authority**

Example: If a spell is set to target anyone with red hair, then blondes cannot be targeted. The spell would also include those who had dyed their hair to make it red. Redheads who had dyed their hair black would not be affected, since they now had black hair. But if any hair on their bodies was still red, then they could be affected.

This law is also about setting limits on the magical effects. If there are no limits the spell may try to do too much and be spread too thin. Also, the more clear-cut and specific the targeting is, the easier it is for the spell to do its job.

7. The Law of Resistance/Immunity: In a given grouping of similar beings or things, some individuals will be more resistant to a given effect or spell than others. **Authority**

Example: In a herd of cows, all of which appear to be similar, some will be more easily affected by elf-shot than others.

Another example of authority. You will not be able to affect things you don't have proper authority over. Some things will resist because they have more authority than you do.

8. Law of Perversity: If something can possible go wrong, there is a good chance that it will. **Authority**

Example: A lightning spell may go awry or may ricochet back upon the hapless spellcaster who hadn't plugged loopholes or been careful about details in his spell. This may also result in interesting, bizarre, or lethal effects upon the named targets or innocent, unfortunate bystanders, trees, buildings, etc.

This law reflects on the authority of the spellcaster and punishes those who have made mistakes (thus abusing or mis-using their authority).

9. The Law of Deflection: Also called "the Medusa Effect." Here' one spellcaster may reflect an incoming spell back upon its caster via a previous activation of a mirroring spell, charm, or amulet. **Authority**

Example: If one spellcaster sends shot at another person, animal, or structure which had superior wards installed against that particular spell, then the shot would either ricochet back upon the sender or scatter out to secondary targets.

If the protection of the target is strong enough it has the authority to repel the spell being sent against it. If your authority isn't greater than the target you will fail. This is similar to the Low of Resistance/Immunity.

Organizing these Laws of Magic into categories formalizes the concepts of Resonance and Authority can offer new insights in the laws and how they operate and how they can be exploited by the magician.

In Conclusion

Overall, Rún Valdr gives you great tools to do magic. Tools that can help you be specific in where you send energy, tools to act as short cuts to save time, and tools that are always at your disposal. Looking at theory behind magic can give you insights on how to make Rún Valdr work better for your own magical practice.

Chapter Seven
Magical Objects

Creating magical objects is surprisingly easy using Rún Valdr. Essentially you are attuning objects to perform specific tasks. When I say magical object I mean some physical object that you set up to give off energy to accomplish specific goals. This practice is common in terms of magical work. I'm sure most who have some experience with magic are familiar with charging objects for magical purposes. I myself have charged many crystals and other things over the years.

The advantage of using a magical object is that it is always working for you. It is not a spell that has a time limit or would be single use only. Since the magical object will always be working, you need to think about what kind of effect you will want. The desired goal for a magical working may not translate well to an object and vice versa.

One thing that is also common with normal magical or charged objects is the need to periodically recharge them as they lose their charge over time. Being lazy, and laziness being just as good as necessity in terms of invention, I found a way with Rún Valdr to avoid the need to constantly charge your magical objects.

By using a combination of object specific attuning symbols, other object specific symbols and permanent energy conduits, you can create objects that have a constant supply of energy. This creates a self powered magical object that needs no further charging.

When I first started using Rún Valdr to create magical objects I would just do a normal attunement. With all the different symbols and runes available in Rún Valdr you have a wide range of tools to use to create the exact effect you want. Using a normal attunement worked great and was simple enough.

However, I noticed that the objects would lose their charge. I went to Odin with the problem and He gave me a specific attunement symbol to use for objects as well as a sealing symbol to be used for objects. I also had the idea of a symbol similar to Reloxon that could be used as a conduit between an energy source and the object. Thus Reloxoné was born.

This worked better, but even though the charge lasted longer, the energy still diminished. I then received Relanor which creates a permanent energy conduit. This did the trick and the objects maintained their energy. Other object specific came later to round out the whole process.

Because you can have a large number of symbols to attune into an object, I recommend first thinking about what symbols and/or runes you will be needing to use for your object. Then write down these symbols/runes so that you will handy. It's quite frustrating to be almost done with the attunement of your object only to find that you have forgotten a symbol.

There are several object specific symbols. These are Haxo, Grimbol (for objects), Turan, Relanor, Dorvin, Naglaish and Kremen. These symbols are specifically designed to work with objects; although I would argue that Relanor, Dorvin, Naglaish and Kremen can be used with people as well. However these symbols are great for making magical objects.

To briefly go over these symbols again, Haxo is used to awaken the object, to make it more self-aware. Grimbol is used for the actual attunement. Turan is used specifically to seal an attunement on an object. Relanor is used as a permanent conduit between the object and a power source and is extremely important in creating magical objects. This allows the object to be a self powered magical object. Dorvin is used to make the object an energy battery. Naglaish is used so that any energy stored becomes condensed and thus stronger. Kremen is very important in that is will allow the object to radiate its energy outward into the world so that it can affect things around it.

As mentioned you are basically attuning objects to perform specific tasks and this process can be broken down into several steps.

Step 1: First, you want to determine clearly what you want the object to do. Do you want a healing crystal, a stone to ward your property, to give your car better protection, to create a servitor? The list of possible items and uses is practically limitless. I've attuned my contact lenses to help with eye health and to help my vision. I've attuned food to make it more nourishing and healing. Ingesting magical food is a cornerstone of several religions. Not only the Christian faith, but this was also found in the various Pagan Mystery Religions (which is technically where Christianity got it).

Step 2: The second step is to figure out what object you want to use. Pretty much any object can be made into a magical item. If you plan on making a lot, you may want to keep a list handy describing each item and what it's supposed to do. I've attuned a lot of those tumbled semi-precious stones, but can't remember what each one is supposed to do anymore.

Step 3: The next step is to wake the object up using Haxo. I usually combine Haxo with an activation symbol to give it power. This awakening of the object is so that it will be more aware and able to perform its function better. This concept is similar to painting eyes on boats, in some cultures, so that they can see where they are going.

Once the object is awakened, I then speak to it, usually out loud, explaining the function I would like it to do. I also tell the object that I will now give it tools to use to perform its function.

Step 4: At this point I do an attunement on the object, using the attunement symbol specific for objects instead of the one for people. The only real difference is that, as each symbol/rune is attuned to the object I will tell it what each one is for.

Step 5: After all the symbols are attuned, but before you seal the attunement, it is time to connect the object to a power source. I tend to use the sun a lot as a good general purpose power source. For an object dedicated to meditative or trance journey work I would use the moon. For grounding, I would use the earth. You could also use a galaxy, or symbols representing the elemental planes. I would not use any Deity as a power source as you would be draining Their power. I would see this, at best, being extremely rude, and at worst, theft which might lead one to be punished.

To use Relanor, see the object in one of the circles with the other circle around your power source. The line in the middle can stretch as far as you need to wherever the power source is. Once this link has been established, use Dorva to start the energy flow. Since Relanor sets up a permanent power conduit, this energy flow will be continuous. Your magical item will have all the energy it needs to perform its function. You can also use Lugar to increase or decrease the size of the conduit to allow more or less energy to come through into the object.

As I already discussed in Chapter Three, I used to feel that this energy flow should be a one-way flow of energy from the power source into the object. But I found that it is better to see Relanor as a two-way conduit to encourage a full flow of energy, much as you see with electric circuits. After some experiments the energy flow does seem stronger than with a one-way conduit. I leave it to you to experiment further, but I strongly recommend a two-way flow. But either way you should try to concentrate on feeling a strong sense of this energy moving into and powering the object. Let the object feel powerful in your hands, an object of power and potency.

Step 6: After the link to the power source is established it is time for the attunement sealing. Use Turan to seal the attunement on the object and the whole process is complete. Your magical item is ready for use.

To sum up the process:

1. Plan out what you want the object to do and what symbols/runes you will need.
2. Use Haxo and an activation symbol to "awaken" the object.
3. Tell it what its purpose will be.
4. Perform an attunement, telling the object what each symbol/rune will be used for.
5. Connect item to a power source using Relanor.
6. Seal the attunement.

Once you have your object you can carry it around to gain the effect, or depending on how you set it up, it could be placed in a central location to work on the area around it. Typically it easiest to make the magical object something you can wear, or keep in your pocket. Of course attuning your car and house can be just as effective.

I find that objects don't need a whole lot of prep time. Some traditions would have you cleanse and/or purify any object you would charge for magical needs. While this may be a good idea, for Rún Valdr I am on the fence as to whether this is needed. I can see the need to remove any other influences that may be attached to an object but it will not impair the effectiveness of any object attunement if you don't cleanse the object first.

If you want to purify any object first, I would suggest that you use Grija and Idunnath to purify and to restore the object to a pristine state. Again, when using these symbols for a working on the object, the intention is the removal of any previous influence that may be on that object.

In terms of what kind of objects you can attune the options are limitless. You can attune your jewelry, your clothing, your house, your car, your food, your property (the land you live on), your computer, etc.

Spirit Servitors

I would like to spend some time discussing a subject that can offer you a great tool to use in your magical practice. It is one that fits well with the tools that Rún Valdr gives you. I am talking about servitors. This is essentially creating an energy being who then goes out and does the work for you. The advantage of a servitor is that unlike an object, servitors can move and go places. They can be sent to help someone far away where, by definition, objects must remain local.

Traditional methods have you carefully delineate the time frame for the existence of your servitor so that it dissolves, or disappears after the work is done. The reason is that any being needs energy to exist. If your servitor is going to hang around, it needs to get energy from somewhere. This could lead it to try to suck energy from people. I now wonder if many poltergeist phenomenon are not just rogue servitors trying to raise and drain energy from people. The servitor is normally fed enough energy to get the work done and then when the work is done, or when some pre-determined period of time it has elapsed dissolves. For instance you could have it active from full moon to full moon or until the work is complete.

I recall a series of books from my youth where you are taught techniques for creating "genies" who then do magical work for you; getting a new job, healing, etc. This is essentially the same as creating servitors. The author is Robert Ferguson and the books I had were *Universal Mind: New way to Mystic Power* and *Prosperity and Psychic Telemetry: New Key to Health, Wealth, and Perfect Living*. I found these books while still in high school and found them to be fascinating. Sure the book promised a lot and some of the instructions were contradictory, but it opened me up to the possibility of using magic for practical needs.

These books had you create genies representing the thing you wanted. A large man in armor, for example, if you needed protection, or a rich banker with pockets overflowing with money if you needed money, etc. You would call them forth in your mind's eye, converse with them and let them know what you wanted. Then you sent them on their way. The usual things applied, about them not harming anyone, etc. You also gave them instructions for how long they should be working.

I had the idea that with Reloxoné and Relanor you could easily insure that any servitor becomes connected to a power source and could get all the energy they needed to do their work. If you are making a temporary servitor that is only lasting a relatively short time, you would use Reloxoné. If you want to create a permanent servitor that will always be around, then use Relanor. Plus you can use Reloxon as a timing device to limit the lifetime of the servitor.

If you decide to create a permanent servitor, you should think a great deal about it first. You will be creating something that will be sticking around for a long time. Will the servitor outlive its usefulness? Will it be serving a function that can and should be done on a continuous basis forever? If the answer is no, then don't make a permanent servitor. In most cases a temporary servitor will be enough.

I was going to give instructions on creating a servitor, but I find much better instructions can be found in Damon Brand'sk book, *Magickal Servitors*. I would recommend that if you are interested in servitors to get his book. The author mentions that connecting servitors to generic energy sources has limited use as they respond best to personal energy of the magician. You feed them with your own emotions and paying attention to them. In light of this further information, feeding would still need to be done periodically, but I see the benefits of connecting a servitor to a power supply to make them stronger.

Whether one is making magical objects or powering servitors Rún Valdr, again, provides useful tools for you to have fun with.

Chapter Eight
Advanced Techniques

Once you have mastered the basics of Rún Valdr you will be ready for more advanced techniques. These techniques go beyond what have been covered so far in several different ways, from new ways of using symbols to an entirely different method of using Rún Valdr. The advanced ideas can be broken down into four sections: Deity Symbols, Auto-Symbols, Rún Valdr level Two, and Experimental symbols. Deity Symbols are symbols gained from various Deities, representing Their presence. Auto-Symbols are symbols that continue to work after they have been attuned. Rún Valdr level Two is an entirely new system of Rún Valdr. Experimental symbols are extra symbols that are not quite ready to be included with the canon symbols.

Deity Symbols

Deity symbols was an idea that came to me while doing lots of mental journeys to visit Odin and Freyja to get the various symbols and techniques for Rún Valdr. I realized the value of having a symbol that represents the presence of a specific Deity. Then when one uses that symbol one would be filled with Their presence. Not only is this useful in a devotional way, it would also have side benefits as well.

First one would be able to make a direct connection to a Deity and thus more easily build a relationship with that Deity. It is very pleasant to be in the presence of one's Deity, as the love and care that They feel for us is great. Deity Symbols makes it quite easy to achieve this connection and is worth the effort to gain the symbol. Secondly, being that close to someone that powerful would surely rub off on you, helping one to become greater as well. A Deity symbol then becomes a tool of self development as well as a tool of Divine connection. I figure the purpose of all religion is to give us tools to access the Divine. Deity symbols makes this a much easier task. Of all the Rún Valdr symbols, Deity symbols are something that I do not recommend people share with others. Each symbol represents your personal connection to that Deity, not a general connection. It would not be appropriate to share the symbols with others.

I've spent some time already discussing trance journey work. I recommend that you visit your Deities and ask Them for symbols to represent Their presence. When I ask for a symbol They draw it for me hanging in the air in front of me. After memorizing the symbol (or most likely taking time to write it down then and there), I ask for the name of the symbol. They usually have to repeat it many times until I can "hear" it. I then write down the name as well. Taking time to write down stuff while doing trance journey can break the experience for many, and this may take some practice for you to mentally move in and out of the trance journey like that. Otherwise, memorize the best you can and write the information down after you return.

Deity symbols do not have names per se. The name of the Deity is the name of the symbol, and you would use the Deities name when doing the symbol activation. I see the Deity symbol large within me, then I do the symbol activation. I am then immediately filled with Their presence. It is great to use during devotional rites. This is not a possession type experience, although it could be used in such a purpose if you wanted to. It really is a wonderful experience. What I find remarkable is how clearly you can feel different energy from each Deity. That is, Odin feels very different from Freyja or Balder. Even Freyja and Freyr feel different even though there are great similarities.

Deity symbols are something I encourage everyone to try. The benefits are immense. Not only will you grow closer to your Deity, but will in turn benefit from Their presence.

Auto Symbols

Auto symbols are symbols that once attuned, keep working. This may be another example of my laziness, but I thought it might be really useful to not have to think about a symbol working but to have it just be there continuously doing its thing. To be fair I've never really been happy with the results of auto symbols. As a whole it is not an idea that has worked out as well as I hoped. They seem to work for a while and then fade away. I have worked at improving things and even came up with an alternate attunement system that I will share, but still I'm not happy with the results. Maybe I'm missing something. Maybe I'm trying to reach beyond the capability of the system. Maybe it just needs a lot more work. Either way I still think the underlying idea behind auto symbols is pretty cool. I would encourage readers to work with this. Perhaps news eyes will come up with some solution that works better.

The problem, similar with maintaining a charge on magical objects is that the symbols lose effectiveness over time. There a few things I've done to help. One is to come up with a special attunement for auto symbols and the other is a symbol for permanence of action.

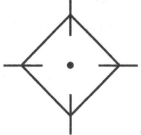

Ganahir - attunement

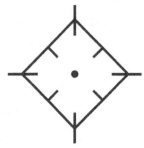

Goshtor - Sealing

Jarnik - Permanency of action.

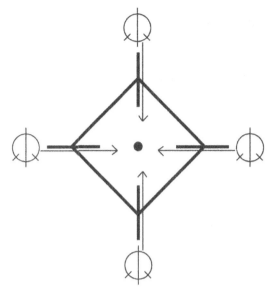

Figure 1

The attunement process is rather different than the normal Rún Valdr attunement. You start with Ganahir centered on the person's second chakra. The symbol is seen as very big. Now for each symbol you will be attuning, see it smaller at each corner of Ganahir, top, bottom, right and left, as shown in the picture above. Do the symbol activation and then see each of the four symbols crash into the center dot (Figure 1). Now use Jarnik over Ganahir. Jarnik's is for permanency of action, that is, it will keep some action going continuously. The intention is that the symbol you just attuned with Ganahir be permanent and eternal.

Now it is time to seal the symbol. See Goshtor over the person and Ganahir. Do the symbol activation and feel energy flow in through the lines at the top, bottom, and sides and then get locked in the diagonal directions. If everything works out the symbol will work continuously within you giving you the benefit of the symbol all the time. You could also do a normal working and then seal with Jarnik to make the working permanent.

Here are a few auto symbols that I have received to get you started.

 **Tormin - To make one's hair very soft**

 **Trellheim (gold) - To increase one's healing rate to a dramatic degree**

 **Valna (gold) - To increase ability to learn new things in general**

Rún Valdr Level Two

I really hesitate to say this is Rún Valdr level two, as it is not really a more powerful method, nor is it the next logical step for Rún Valdr to go. This system uses two symbols and an unusual attunement process. The two symbols are the main symbol which is used for the working and the symbol used to seal the attunement. There is no attunement symbol at all. The system is very third chakra oriented. This was revealed to me by the Goddess Sif, Thor's wife and so has no connection to Odin and Freyja. It is a more meditative/transformative practice rather than the more active use of energy one normally finds with Rún Valdr. Essentially you are attuned to a symbol which you then program, more or less like Shai Nal and then meditate on the second symbol, thus gaining the properties of that symbol.

Gana - Main working symbol

This is the main symbol you will be using for this system. During the working it will be visualized centered on the third chakra, at the diaphragm.

Torna - Attunement Sealing

This symbol is only used to seal the attunement.

During the attunement process you will be repeating the name "Gana" until the attunement is done. Start by visualizing a connection, like a beam of light, between the Sun and the Earth. Then visualize a connection between the Sun and the person being attuned (this could be yourself). Then visualize a connection between the Earth and the person. You will basically end up with a triangle. Sun to earth, sun to person and earth to person. Next visualize energy filling the body, spreading out from the third chakra. After the person's body is filled let the energy expand beyond the body to form the shape of Gana. After this seal the attunement with Torna.

To use the system, visualize Gana within yourself centered on the third chakra. You do not have to do a symbol activation for Gana, just visualize it within you. Then choose a Rún Valdr symbol or a rune to use and picture it at the center of Gana. Do a symbol activation for the chosen symbol/rune and just meditate on the symbol. The symbol/rune will replace the dot in Gana.

Example of Gana in use with Freyl-Tay symbol.

This use of Rún Valdr is, as I have said, more meditative than the regular use of Rún Valdr. The idea is to absorb and take on the characteristics of the symbol you use inside of Gana. When done you can just let the image of Gana and the symbol you are using fade away. Or you can be more formal and use Tunai to seal the working.

Experimental Symbols

These are essentially symbols that need more work to be useful. Because they need more work, they are not included in the Rún Valdr canon of symbols. The ideas sounded cool, so I asked for symbols for these things. I'm including them here so that people may experiment with them. They are used like the regular Rún Valdr symbol, by programming them into Shai Nal. The exception would be Sav Nal, which is like Shai Nal, and Grannath, which is a new attunement symbol.

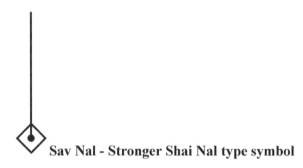

Sav Nal - Stronger Shai Nal type symbol

Pronunciation: Sahv-Nahl

I asked Odin for a stronger Shai Nal like symbol and was given Sav Nal.

This symbol is another attempt to squeeze more power out of Rún Valdr. This time it is a modification to the working symbol instead of the activation symbol. I figured that the energy used in a working is being run through the working symbol, so different working symbols would yield different results. A symbol designed to handle more energy may have more dramatic results. This symbol should give quicker and stronger results than Shai Nal. I like this symbol and use it all the time.

Use it instead of Shai Nal and see how results vary.

Grannath - Stronger attunement symbol

Pronunciation: Græ-nath (the gra is the same as in the word "granite")

I received this symbol from Odin. I had been thinking of how different symbols might change the attunement process and asked for a new attunement symbol. Grannath was the result.

This symbol is an attunement symbol, but offers a deeper experience. I have an idea different attunements can unlock different strength levels of the energy that can be channeled. The look of this symbol is more appropriate in my mind for an attunement. The dot at the end suggests a concentration of might and the main goal is to lock in all the runes and symbols into the second chakra. The diagonal lines seem to offer extra energy coming into the system. I like using this attunement symbol. For me it has a nice, solid feel.

This symbol can be used for attunements on people, as well as for objects. I would encourage experimentation and see how the results vary from the Grimbol attunement symbol.

Skowron - To create resonance

Pronunciation: Skow (like cow)-Ron

I got this symbol from Odin and Freyja. I felt, based on the magical theory information They gave, that having some mechanism for gaining resonance was important. It should be noted that the two lines between the triangles are two lines, not a solid bar.

As discussed in the section on magic, being able to create resonance with something is useful in trying to change it or work with it. Skowron can be used to gain resonance. It can be used similar to Reloxon, where you are in one of the triangles and the target is in the other. This could be you gaining resonance with something else, or it could be resonance between two other people or things.

I could see this being used not only for magic, but to help in relationships in general.

Garnas - For Potency

Pronunciation: Gar-Nahss

This symbol came from Sif. I had asked for a symbol to represent potency, and this is what She gave me.

Potency in this case is not dealing with one's ability to procreate. Instead it is a measure of one's effectiveness and being able to get things done. For example, Superman could be seen as extremely potent as he could stop volcanoes, and other natural disasters. Any working can benefit from extra potency.

This is to be used to add extra weight to your workings, whether for magical purposes, or healing.

Karanal - To have children

Pronunciation: Kar-ah-nahl

I believe this symbol was given to me without my asking for it. I can't recall how I got it. It may be that I was called to draw it, and then later asked Odin and Freyja what it was for.

I imagine this symbol would be for all stages of having children from conception to birth. It could help with fertility issues or with women prone to miscarriage. I really have only had cause to use this symbol once and the results were not immediately clear or positive. The woman had a miscarriage not long after the symbol was used (within hours). She has since given birth to two healthy children, but there is no way to know if Karanal had anything to do with either situation.

The symbol should be used while trying to conceive and then throughout the pregnancy on a regular basis.

Fire in the Head (gold color only) - Creativity? Eloquence?

This symbol came from the Irish God Lugh. I had visited Him to gain a Deity Symbol since he is the Tribal Father God figure in my ADF Grove. Lugh shared this symbol with me without much in the way of explanation.

Traditionally Fire in the Head meant creativity or verbal eloquence, so I will go with this for the meaning of the symbol. This symbol also didn't get a formal name either. I imagine that this symbol would be good for public speaking, or when undertaking creative endeavors. Or even when seeking inspiration in general.

I'm of the opinion that this symbol would be best for inspiration, or eloquence. Perhaps you could attune your keyboard or pen/pencil to help with the flow of creativity.

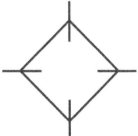

Tor Nal - Synchronicity

Pronunciation: Tor Nahl

There was a series of symbols where I kind of put out an intention for something and just felt compelled to draw symbols. This is one of them.

242

This symbol is kind of like Skowron. Where Skowron creates specific resonance patterns between specific things, Tor Nal would be more of a general resonance with the Universe kind of thing. The idea is that when using Tor Nal, things naturally go your way because you are in tune with the Universe.

The idea is that when using this symbol, things would flow in a person's life. Things just work out and everything just falls into place. You are always in the right place at the right time.

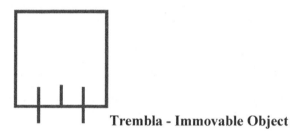 **Trembla - Immovable Object**

Pronunciation: Trem-Blah

I got this symbol from Yggdrasil. There was a similar symbol received the same way as Tor Nal, but I wanted something less random, and asked for this.

This symbol and Zorman are wild kind of experiments. One hears stories of the Unstopple Force meeting the Immovable Object and the speculations as to what would happen. What kind of situations would require such solidity so as to be immovable? The absolute manifestation of will? To keep something from changing? To protect something?

I suppose magically Trembla can be used to create a "fixed" point that is a thing that must manifest because it is immovable.

Zorman - Unstoppable Force

Pronunciation: Zor-mahn

This symbol also came from Yggdrasil, in the same way as Trembla, above. Like Trembla, there had also been a previous version.

This has a bit of wild speculation to it, as with Trembla. Unlike Trembla, I can see this symbol being used to add a lot of force behind whatever it may be that you are trying to do. If this symbol works, it could be truly awesome in its force. But then again, one does not want to kill a mosquito with a sledgehammer or a nuclear weapon. If it works it should be used responsibly.

On a distressing note, I just found out that this symbol has been used by white supremacist groups. I found out about this years after getting the symbol. Hopefully this will not cause a problem, but is something to keep in mind. I had no previous knowledge of this same symbol being used anywhere else before receiving it.

Overall, Trembla and Zorman may just be fanciful thinking on my part. I have to admit to being skeptical as to how much force could be brought to bear using Zorman, or how much Trembla can really withstand. However I am fascinated by the potential of these two symbols. It is this kind of speculative use of Rún Valdr that pushes the envelope of what is possible and is necessary to make further progress. Such efforts may not always work, but the seeking can be its own rewards. As the saying goes, nothing ventured, nothing gained.

244

 **Gord - Aids in manifestation**

Pronunciation: Gord

I received this symbol from Sif.

Similar in function to the rune Isa, Gord is to help manifest things. When I got this symbol the idea was to help manifest one's magical working or desires. However, as I write this it occurs to me that it could be used in cases of summoning of spirits to help with physical manifestation. This is really the holy grail of grimoire magic, and typically is unrealistic. But with this symbol? Who knows?

It also might be combined with astral projection work to enhance the experience. I know when doing trance journey work the whole thing can be kind of like a heavy daydream rather than a true out of body experience.

There are several symbols that can be used for manifestation kind of effects. Garnas, for potency, Zorman and Gord all could be used for similar purposes. Garnas and Zorman seem very similar in function, which is adding strength and potency to a working. Gord seems to be about actual materialization into form. Gord may share a closer similarity to Trembla if looked at in strict terms of manifestation only.

 **Dorval - Brings down divine might**

Pronunciation: Dor-Vahl

I got this symbol from Odin. This symbol had an unusual beginning. There was a time when I entertained the idea of channeling Deities and thought having a sequence of symbols to use might help the process. Dorval to bring down divine might would be the literal act of bringing the Deity to the physical world so that They could inhabit a person's body for awhile. The whole channeling idea never took off, but the idea of bringing divine might into a situation does seem attractive.

Unlike Grishtor which makes things holy, Dorval would seem to imply bringing down divine might for a purpose. Perhaps when dealing with negative entities, or cases of hauntings. It would be used in cases where you would want a touch of divine energy into what you are doing.

 Sambor - Still the mind and screen out subjective elements

Pronunciation: Sam Bor

I got this symbol from Seidh, a Chieftain of Sif. I wanted a symbol to help with trance journey work.

This symbol was sought to overcome, at least to some degree, the natural tendency for trance journey work to be very subjective. A lot of trance work involves stilling the "chattering monkey" so that the subjective can be pushed aside for a little while. As mentioned before, subjective ideas and thoughts can get in the way of trance journey work. This is an attempt to help with that process of keeping trance journey work as objective as possible.

I would use this symbol as part of a magical object used for trance journey work. This object could be an item of clothing; bracelet, cloak, necklace, hat, etc.

Chowron - Support and strength for infrastructures

Pronunciation: Chow (rhymes with cow) Ron

I got this symbol from Odin. I felt a need for a symbol to improve infrastructures in general.

There is a symbol for opening and closing, which can work great on opening up blockages. There is a symbol for channeling energy to insure good energy flow. However I realized that there was not a symbol for supporting the energy pathway network itself. Chowron's function is to strengthen and support the pathway infrastructure, making sure that it is strong enough to handle increased loads. I imagine that this symbol would work on any pathway, whether cardio-vascular, neural, psychic, electrical, or even connections/pathways between people.

I feel this symbol is good for any healing work, especially work dealing with the body's infrastructure. I would also use it working where one is trying to increase one's power. Opening up oneself to more power is worthless unless the underlying infrastructure can support the increase.

As stated already, these symbols are experimental and need to be tested. I encourage the reader to use these symbols and do your own experimentation.

This also concludes the Advanced Rún Valdr section. Rún Valdr has many facets and I hope you have enjoyed this deeper look inside.

Chapter Nine
Final Thoughts

The journey of Rún Valdr, although by no means complete, has been rewarding beyond measure. My gratitude and appreciation to my Gods know no bounds. Through Them, this wonderful system has come to fruition. The creation of Rún Valdr has been a great exercise in trance journey work and the value of bringing knowledge from the Other Worlds.

Sometimes I'm tempted to think that I just made it all up, that my trance journeys are not true out-of-body experiences. They seem, as I stated already, to be like heavy daydreams. All experiences of this type are heavily influenced and filtered by the self. If I and someone else were to go on a trance journey to visit Freyja in Asgard, I'm sure each of us would see a different Asgard, a different looking Freyja, a different time of day etc. If we asked the same question we might even get two completely different answers. However, if both of us had gained some skill in trance work, there would most likely be details that overlapped. This is where truth is found.

Granted even though most everyone may have similar experiences, there is always that one who falls down a hole and is chased by flying vampire rabbits and are forced to shoot Hindu Gods with mortar shells while singing Italian opera. Obviously this person was nowhere close to being on the same page as everyone else. Is that okay? Well from a purely personal way, sure. They had an experience. But if you are looking at trying to get a group consensus about something, and/or to gain objective information, then no.

At this point, you really have to ask what is subjective and what is objective when dealing with trance journeys. I'm not convinced that such trance journey can ever by truly free of subjectivity, but one can strive to reach a point where objective information can be gained. I'm reminded of the role-playing game Shadowrun. One class, or profession, is the decker, a specialized computer hacker who mentally projects themselves inside computer systems. There is no end of the variety of user interfaces that can be chosen. For example one person could have an old west theme, where the anti-hacking programs trying to stop them could look like a Sherriff and deputies, the goal could be in an old time safe inside a bank. On the other side, the hacker could look like a typical Old West bandit. Or there could be a samurai theme, or a space theme. And they all could be mixed up. Two different deckers could approach the same target and see totally different things, but the defenses and the goal are all real in an objective way. It doesn't matter if I'm storming a medieval castle, an old west bank, a modern skyscraper, or a space station and it doesn't matter if I'm breaking into a locked chest, an old time safe, a modern safe, or a fancy computer, I'm still going to get the latest plans of project X from company Y.

Perhaps trance journeys are like that where we all have our own subjective user interfaces to deal with. The exact details will change, person to person, but there are still objective truths to be had. The trick is to find the objective truth from the subjective information projected by our own user interface. Keep in mind that, as humans, we have our own insights and I have great faith in the transcendent brilliance of our subconscious and our ability to be creative. However, there is a time for subjective content and a time to set that aside. The symbol Sambor mentioned in the last chapter is an attempt to weed out that subjective stuff that at times is pure nonsense that gets in the way of actually getting outside your own head and into the larger world around you.

That said, Rún Valdr works, which leads me to believe that there is some objective truth behind it. If it was all in my head, then the system wouldn't work, right? I'm sure that if someone else had gone to Odin and Freyja for a similar system the symbols would look different, the attunement would be different, and the working would be different. Would it still work? Most likely yes.

Regardless of the origin, Rún Valdr above all else is a system of magic, a set of tools for you to use. This system can be adapted to a wide range of circumstances and situations. It is my hope that Rún Valdr becomes as big a part of your life as it has in mine.

I welcome folks to visit the Rún Valdr website. You will find materials such as the quick start sheet as well as a list of extra symbols.

http://uberrod.com/runvaldr01.html

Go forth and do the will of Odin and Freyja.

Appendix A
Rún Valdr History

One of the reasons this book is necessary is so that an accurate and clear history of the system is recorded. I wanted to avoid the mess that current Reiki practitioners are faced with, regarding their history. People shouldn't have to guess at my motives or methods. Nor do grandiose claims need to be created regarding how Rún Valdr came to be. It's not that Reiki is not good. To the contrary, Reiki is wonderful. However, the history is muddled at best and this is an injustice to the practitioners of the system and could deter some talented people from taking up the system.

Some of this information has been covered earlier in the book so bear with me as things get repeated.

First you should know a little about me and where I'm coming from. I am currently a polytheistic Pagan and my personal Gods are from the Norse Pantheon. Odin and Freyja are my Patrons as well as Sif, and Idunna and it was information gained from Them, combined with ideas I had while learning Reiki that evolved into the system I call Rún Valdr.

When I say I am Pagan, I mean that I worship the old Gods that were worshipped in Europe before the coming of Christianity. Another way to say it would be that I follow an indigenous religion of Europe. But it gets more complicated than that. I am a member of Ár nDraíocht Féin: A Druid Fellowship (ADF). However, ADF is not just a Celtic Druid organization, but encompasses all Indo-European cultures. Given this and the fact that my personal Gods are Norse, I hesitate to call myself a Druid (which is a Celtic term). But ambiguous religious identity aside, I look to the Norse Gods and it was They who helped me develop Rún Valdr.

And when I say I'm polytheistic it doesn't mean that I'm involved in a relationship with multiple people, it means that I accept that there are many Deities in existence. I may only worship a few of them, but I know that there are many others out there. Just like there are many countries and cultures in the world. Just because I'm American doesn't mean that I don't believe that Taiwan exists.

But it was actually another Deity that first set me on the path that would eventually lead me to Rún Valdr. Before I joined ADF, and living in Detroit, I was fairly close to Brid, or Brigit, Irish Goddess of Hearth, Healing and Blacksmithing. In the nearby town of Ann Arbor, a couple was running a Reiki healing circle. I attended and felt the wonderful energy of Reiki first hand. I had to learn this for myself and eventually got my first attunement in Sacred Path Reiki in the early part of September of 1996. My teachers came up with their own name since the system was modified in that it had some symbols at first level. This is highly unusual as typically all symbol work begins with the second level of Reiki.

However during their first level Reiki attunements, these new symbols came to my teachers and thus they felt it was appropriate to incorporate them in the first level of the Reiki they taught. The symbols were for opening and closing the aura and were useful in healings and attunements as well as other aspects of healing work such as pain management and shutting out negative influences. It was mostly used to open up the aura so there would be a greater degree of communication between practitioner and the client. It allowed the person being worked on to have an easier time with the exchange of energy.

I can tell you that the attunement was an amazing experience. I felt all sorts of strange and wondrous energies moving through me during the attunement. I learned the hand positions and how to use Reiki. It was wonderful, and I wanted more. I had an almost overpowering urge to learn more Reiki. Looking back, I feel it was Brid who was pushing me. It really was a burning desire or obsession to gain the highest levels of attunement to Reiki and is hard to describe unless you've been through a similar experience.

It is said that after an attunement there is a 21 day adjustment period. Since the attunement opens up and prepares the upper chakras, this can lead to any negative energy being broken up and processed. An adjustment can have all sorts of physical manifestations. A fellow Reiki student had a film that kept forming over her eyes. She said she could peel it off in sheets. After the 21 days, the problem cleared up and afterwards she reported that everything looked new again. If she walked into a room in her home, one she had been in hundreds of times, it was like she was walking into it for the first time. Personally, I didn't have any manifestations at all during my 21 day adjustment period. Maybe it was all the other energy work I had been doing. Maybe I'm just dense.

After my attunement it was like a new world had opened up to me. I could heal now! But it wasn't enough, and 21 days after my first level attunement, I received my second level attunement. This attunement felt different, more powerful than the first. I remember sitting there with my eyes closed, yet I could feel my teacher as he moved around us. His energy felt so clear to me. After the attunement I learned the different symbols that one learns with the second level.

If a new world opened up after the first attunement, it was nothing compared to the second level Reiki attunement. The energy flow was so much stronger, and I could work at a distance. The amazing thing is that the next day, I got an e-mail from a gentleman in France whom I had never met before and knew nothing about. His friend needed some healing but he was too far away and didn't have a way to travel to her. He was apparently only level one Reiki. So he wanted me to do a distance healing for her since he wasn't able to. I was happy to help out. But what really struck me was how did he know I was a second level Reiki practitioner? How did he know who I was in the first place? There was absolutely no way for anyone to know, except for my immediate friends and family. It was one of the weirder things that have happened to me.

I received my Master level Reiki attunement during August of 1998. I was a member of ADF by then. The attunement was a wonderful and magical experience that I will always treasure. My teachers devoted a whole weekend for the attunement and training and even rented out a small campground north of Ann Arbor, Michigan. Sadly the camp is no longer there as it has been sold to a private party. The camp was off a small lake and the scene was idyllic. The fee I paid for the attunement went towards the cost of the camp and to help pay the assistants who prepared our food. There were two other students besides myself.

I arrived Friday excited and helped my teachers make a sweat lodge. My teachers were also involved in Native American practices and felt that incorporating a sweat lodge would be beneficial. This was a great experience in and of itself. I had never done a sweat lodge before and didn't really know what to expect. Well, it was very hot, but energizing as well. The plan was to do the sweat and then have the attunements on the beach which was just outside the sweat lodge.

I was so blown away from the sweat that I didn't feel the attunement at all, much to the dismay of my teachers. They had wanted feedback on how it felt. You really don't feel much when giving a Reiki attunement and I'm sure my teachers felt a disappointed that we didn't feel anything ourselves.

Then on Saturday the training began. We learned the basics of giving an attunement, what all the master level symbols were and how to use them. We practiced on each other and I learned a lot. The combination of being in a tranquil setting, having a whole weekend to learn and practice was amazing. I highly recommend it to everyone.

Then I began teaching others Reiki. I also had a strong inclination towards symbols, and sought out ever more symbols to work with. Runes, in particular, held a fascination since I was starting my relationship with Odin. I began to incorporate runes in my Reiki workings and also to explore and learn about new symbols that others had discovered and were sharing. I wanted to learn more and more symbols. Like the urgent desire to learn Reiki, I had a desire to learn about new symbols. I think I felt that I could do more with more symbols. There were a great many symbols for a great many things. I also learned new traditions of Reiki, both from my teachers and from other folks in exchange for teaching the system I had learned.

Regarding the learning of new Reiki traditions, in the end I became attuned to the master level of about a dozen different Reiki traditions, give or take, each one having new symbols that could do different things. A few, like the Atlantean system were completely different and more complex than any Reiki I had ever learned. But the rest followed the standard formula. You first needed the basic Usui Reiki attunement then you got attuned to the other traditions and these acted as addendums to what you were already doing. All had you use the Usui power symbol to turn things on. None were really independent of the Usui tradition. Except the Atlantean system. I'd go into it but I don't want to confuse you as it is very complicated. Just trust me when I say that this particular system was independent of Reiki. But it was also very complex and very tricky to use. It lacked the simplicity of Reiki and I never really used it at all.

Looking back, (and as I've commented already) you really only need a minimum of symbols when working with Reiki. The power symbol that gave you access to the full amount of Reiki energy the distance symbol so that you could heal/attune someone anywhere and the Master Symbol to do attunements. Anything beyond that is really needless. That statement may offend some, especially Reiki people, but it is objectively true. One must remember that the core of Reiki belief is that you don't really do the work at all. The Reiki energy itself is self-aware and knows what to do and just requires you to be there as the conduit. So having extra symbols really doesn't add much. Intent and turning on the juice is all you really need.

That said, why was I so obsessed with learning more symbols? Why were so many others gaining more and more symbols themselves? I'm not sure. Symbols, especially the kind you find in the various Reiki traditions are powerful representations of abstract ideas and thus powerful tools. Maybe it is an inherent need to order and define things and symbols help us do that. Maybe we, as humans, don't trust the consciousness of Reiki and think we need to interfere and direct it, despite the fact that this idea goes against one of the fundamental principles of Reiki itself.

I wonder now if this desire for more symbols was the influence of Odin. After all, He hung on the World Tree for nine days to learn the secrets of 24 powerful symbols. Of course, I could go on about how inherently magical alphabets are and how important the ability to read and write can be. Writing is an easy way to transmit knowledge. As long as I can remember reading has been important to me. Perhaps Odin has been watching over me longer that I realized.

After achieving master level in Reiki, there was a shift in my Divine relationships. My connection to Brid seemed to wane and it was at this time that I was contacted by Odin. Now I had heard stories that you should be careful about Odin because He tended to betray his followers and set them up for a fall. However, I was very much attracted to the runes. In the end I gave in and I have to say that I have had a very nice, even loving relationship with Him. Other people I've know who have been called to Him have had a rough time with Him and He has demanded much of them. I count myself lucky and blessed to have such a nice relationship.

Later I fell in with Freyja and have been quite happy with Her to guide me. I feel that I have only scratched the surface of what She has to teach me. Still later I made contact with both Idunna and Sif. This change in Deities also pushed me into the Norse religious practices rather than the Celtic that had been so familiar to me up to that time. But I shall be forever grateful to Brid for starting me on the path of energy work.

So there I was, master of a dozen different Reiki traditions, using runes in my healing and calling it Runic Reiki. I found that I could use the runes themselves directly to do Reiki work, even distance work without using any Reiki symbols at all. Algiz acted much like the Power symbol, Isa was good for the distance symbol. It was very interesting to use Reiki without any of the Reiki symbols. I tried a healing on my Reiki teacher using just runes and he said it felt rawer than the normal Reiki energy. I think this discovery was the initial step in creating my own independent system.

Things eventually evolved to where I asked Freyja to give me a symbol to increase my power. I supposed that this would be a good time to mention that at the core of my being was a need to gain power. Not necessarily for evil or selfish purposes, but still I wanted power. That is why I got into the occult in the first place back in high school. I attribute it to me being a Capricorn with Gemini rising. Capricorns, in case you didn't know, are the power brokers of the zodiac. They are all about power and finance and commanding their empire from on high. Geminis are all about the mind and mental pursuits, including magic. I think this combination of traits made me want to have and use power, not necessarily secular or financial power, but magical. And Reiki gave me a good measure of power. I have seen astounding things happen with Reiki and that is gratifying. But obviously I was looking for more. Rún Valdr is one tool in my quest towards this goal.

In college I had started up with ceremonial magick and that was nice and I learned lots. I experimented with various Qi Gong practices (since I have an interest in the martial arts) and also general energy work. After I became Pagan, I gave up on ceremonial magick since it relies heavily on working with the Judeo-Christian Deity. Since I was not Jewish, or Christian, I felt it was not correct for me to continue that work. But I still had a desire for power. What to do?

Getting back to Freyja... I asked Her to give me a symbol to increase my power. She showed me Shai Nal, and it was pretty cool. I could feel that it was a powerful symbol. Freyja referred to it as "bringing the iron within." Later I asked for a symbol for purification and received Grija. One thing led to another and I collected more symbols from both Freyja as well as from Odin. Then I had my bright idea. I could make my own system that was independent of Reiki. I could create a parallel system that incorporated some of the best ideas from Reiki and yet be completely separate from Reiki. That idea really appealed to me.

I should mention the method I used to visit Freyja and Odin to get the symbols and other information used to create Rún Valdr. I suppose to say I astrally projected would be too strong a phrase. I've yet to have a full out of body experience. To say I was merely daydreaming does not nearly go far enough to describe what I was experiencing. Because while I was aware of my body, what I was seeing in my mind's eye had enough objectivity to be more than just a normal kind of daydream. I will use the term trance journey as that is applicable and yet vague enough to not get me into too much trouble with respect to terminology.

The trick to this is to still the mind enough to be open to outside information coming in. The pitfall is that what you are seeing is sometimes just junk coming from one's own subconscious. I think that a lot of people just see and hear what they want to without getting much in the way of objective information. I've heard descriptions of other's experiences that clearly, to me, seemed to be just wish fulfillment or stuff coming only from their own subconscious. For example if, in a group trance journey, we were to visit God X, one person would invariably find God Y and wacky high jinx would ensue and they would find themselves being chased around a Roman temple by green flying monkeys. Never mind that God X, the one trying to be contacted was actually Irish and had no contact with Roman temples, let alone flying monkeys. One must be careful to make sure that the information that is coming through is as objective as possible and be aware that sometimes it will be just junk from the depth of one's self. Such information needs to be verified and examined carefully. Same with any instructions you are given to perform. Just because, in a trance journey, you are told to jump off a bridge doesn't mean you actually should. This brings up the term "mental masturbation" which is just a purely subjective experience that one plays in without much in the way of objective input.

It should be understood that even if one's mind is still and clear as glass and really good objective information is being received it is still being translated through one's own subconscious and conscious mind. Information has to be put into a form that we can understand. So anything you get will be colored by your own perceptions and who you are. An artist is unlikely to get detailed technical information on star ship drives, but an engineer might.

To help with this, group trance journeys can be important. This way multiple people are contacting the same Deity with the same intent or questions to be answered. Then afterwards notes can be compared on what everyone experienced. You will be looking for things that overlap from one person to the next. If out of 10 people, 8 came up with more or less the same information then you can conclude that this is more objective than the radically different ideas the other 2 people received.

What I did was to sit quietly, get centered and then visualized myself standing a few feet away from me. Then I would "transfer" my conscious to this other me. Granted I could still feel my own body, but it was a more formal way of shifting my mental thinking away from my physical self and towards a more spiritual or less physical way of being and looking at things. Once I was established in the other me, which can be weird looking back at yourself, yet still being aware of sitting in one's chair at the same time, I would need a way to travel to the Upper World to speak with my Gods.

I would visualize a pillar of fire roughly the same height as myself. A big part of ADF rituals is opening Portals to act as gates between the realms so that our words and offerings can be seen and heard more clearly by the Gods and other Kindreds and Their presence and blessings could more easily be felt by us. The pillar of fire would act as a gate to the Upper

World so it made a good method to use for my journeys. I would enter the pillar of fire with the intent of visiting my Gods.

This would bring me to the Bifrost Bridge, or the Rainbow Bridge of Norse religious thought. The Bifrost Bridge was a pathway that led to Asgard and the Upper World. I would travel along it and meet Heimdall, who guarded the bridge. After the bridge I would find myself walking the streets of Asgard until I got to Odin's Hall. There I would speak with Him and to Freyja to get symbols.

I found that I would have to listen very carefully to catch what was being said, and it can be challenging "seeing" what is there without trying to make it fit some preconceived idea. It can be rather difficult trying to be objective about what one is experiencing. With practice it gets easier, but you must still be wary of "yourself" getting in the way and tainting the experience with personal bias. It takes constant vigilance. Being able to enter a deep trance, or hypnotic state comes in handy, so that you are not constantly being reminded of your physical self sitting or lying in the physical world. The more focused you can be of the non-physical places you are visiting the better. Your goal is to make these journeys as objective as possible.

When I was ready to come back, I would again visualize a pillar of fire and after entering it, return to my physical body and write down what I had learned. Sometimes I would physically write stuff down as it was being given, which can be kind of distracting. But if I was getting multiple symbols it was the best way to record the information without forgetting anything.

This technique is very useful and easy to modify for groups. Once you have led them to the starting point they can each come back on their own by visualizing the pillar of fire. I have used this with quite a few groups, where I will start them out seeing themselves standing outside their bodies, using the fire to go to a forest clearing with many paths leading away. They are then told to pick a trail to follow and find the Deity they are to talk with. When they are ready to return, they are to picture the pillar of fire and return to their physical bodies on their own.

After reading Trance-Portation by Diana Paxson, I realize that trying to write things down (open your eyes to write while in the middle of trance work) may not be the best thing to do and could lead to problems such as losing parts of your soul. It trance work if you are abruptly brought out of the trance, or jump around without walking the path you originally took, you risk leaving pieces of yourself behind. Same for just leaving through the fire where you are instead of going back to your starting point or home base. I have adjusted how I do things now.

This way seems is much better than having a fully scripted trance journey where what you are doing and seeing is being given to the people every step of the way. I find that I am usually too far behind or too far ahead of the script and then they will tell me I'm supposed to be seeing something that just doesn't fit with what I'm seeing at the time. It can be a pretty frustrating experience. When I lead a group journey, I like let the group go off on their own after giving them the tools to get back on their own. That way it is a much more powerful and personal experience. The only drawback is waiting for everyone to come back so that you can move on. This can be dealt with by waiting sufficiently long enough and then telling everyone it is time to return to their physical bodies. Thus they can wrap things up and return. A good grounding afterwards is always recommended.

It is recommended that you build your own inner places or inner temple (inner hall) to act as starting places to do your inner work. This is great for acting as your home base when doing trance journey work. For instance I have a special room where I always go when doing distance workings and attunements. It is a stone room, or at least tiled in stone. On one side is a stone table with a nice soft mattress where I do workings on people. On the other side is a small bench where I visualize people sitting when I give distance attunements. It is the same room that I always use. I encourage others to do similar things. By building and frequenting a specific place again and again it becomes easier to visit and workings will be more powerful. It is also good visualization practice, where you can not only practice "seeing" but "hearing", "tasting", "smelling" and "touching" with your inner senses. For better practice I would recommend Diana Paxson's book Trance-Portation.

I started to ask for symbols from Odin and Freyja that duplicated certain useful symbols from the various Reiki systems. First was to get something that would do something similar to the power symbol in Reiki. I got Shambul. There was a cool symbol from Seichim Reiki that was used to awaken objects so that they would be more aware and thus able to do their respective jobs better. I asked for a symbol that did that and got not only Haxo, but Haxon as well. I had not asked for Haxon, which awakens animals, and was surprised when Odin added it. I must say that my distance symbol is a heck of a lot simpler than the Reiki one. Those who know the Reiki distance symbol know what I'm talking about. The difference is 22-24 strokes for the Reiki one compared with two circles connected by a line for the Rún Valdr version.

I gathered all the immediately necessary symbols I would need, including the very important attunement symbol. Then I asked Odin to show me how to do an attunement. He told me that there would be just one attunement. At the time, I was comfortable with the Reiki idea of there being three attunements. "Just one?" I asked. "Yes, just one," He answered.

Well okay then. Odin showed me how to do an attunement and this also was much simpler and direct than a Reiki attunement. More will be discussed on attunements in a later chapter.

At last I was ready to put Rún Valdr into a cohesive system. The attunement process was the last piece that was needed. This was November of 2003 when a more or less completed system took shape. I first started teaching Rún Valdr in February of 2004 at ConVocation, a Pagan convention that takes place at the end of February in SE Michigan. One of my students from that class has gone on to attune more people than I have and took to heart when I said to go forth and do the will of Odin and Freyja. The change of the name to Rún Valdr followed soon after.

I have, over the years, refined Rún Valdr and have added to the canon of symbols. I have received many other symbols, but few are ready to be shared with others. Other modifications came later namely Deity symbols and the idea of automatic symbols among other things.

One thing that was sorted out fairly early on was how the system was to be used. It sort of just fell together in a fairly logical way. It became clear that the key to the whole system was Shai Nal and that it would be programmed with other symbols and/or runes. I also didn't really bother with hand positions as found in Reiki. At first I would have someone lay down and put a hand on the top of their head and the other over their second chakra and then proceed with the working, but I began to get a bit uncomfortable since the second chakra is rather close to the various private parts and I didn't want to make anyone uneasy. I found that simply having someone sit in a chair and putting both hands on their shoulders while standing behind them worked fine.

One does not merely turn on Rún Valdr and let in flow like Reiki, one needs to concentrate on Shai Nal throughout the working. This was why programming Shai Nal is important as it is a relatively simple symbol to concentrate on. If one's concentration waivers, then one has to start over. This may seem like a drawback compared to Reiki, but on the other hand, it means that you can direct the energy to go and do what you want. You have a much greater degree of control. You still plug into a greater supply of energy, but you direct it rather than relying on the energy to direct itself.

I am a very visually oriented person, so it is natural that the system given to me would also be highly visual as well. If you have trouble visualizing then I apologize ahead of time.

The next significant thing was changing the name from Runic Reiki to Rún Valdr. I felt it necessary to separate what I was doing from Reiki as it was quickly becoming something altogether different. It was not Reiki with runes that it had started out as. It is an entirely separate system that shares a few traits with Reiki. Rún Valdr was a magical system that can be used for healing rather than a system purely dedicated to healing like Reiki.

This book is an attempt to more fully explain the system and also be a teaching guide for those learning Rún Valdr.

Appendix B
Sif Qi Gong

I asked Sif for a Qi Gong that could be done to gain health benefits and this is what was given to me. If there was a word or phrase in Old Norse for internal energy then I would use it. Until then Qi Gong will have to suffice. The Qi Gong is broken up into three sets of actions, each set containing an energy gathering phase followed by an energy moving phase. I will try to describe the movements as best as I can. Hopefully it will make sense.

There are rules to this Qi Gong practice. When turning to the right you will be breathing in. When turning to the left you will be breathing out. Generally speaking when the arms go up, you will be breathing in and when the arms go down you will be breathing out. When you finish one movement and are ready to start the next, end on the out breath and start the next movement on the in breath.

There is no set speed you should be going, nor is there a specific number of repetitions you need to do. Each movement should be repeated until you feel it is time to move on to the next. Regarding posture you should be standing upright and your feet will be a little more than shoulder width apart, unless otherwise directed.

First Set - Energy Gathering

Start with your forearms pointing away from your body at a ninety degree angle with your palms facing up. The elbows should be tight against the body. The hands should be open and relaxed. During this part you will be concentrating on your hands.

Breathing in, pivot your upper body to the right. The lower body should stay facing forward as much zas possible. Your feet should not move.

Breathing out, pivot your upper body back all the way to the left. Repeat pivoting to the right while breathing in and pivoting to the left while breathing out. Keep this up for as long as you feel it is necessary.

First Set - Energy Movement

As you finish breathing out after being fully pivoted to the left, you breathe in, turn facing forward and bring your arms down to your sides.

As you continue to breathe in, raise your arms up, palms up, keeping them extended out to the side of your body, rather than bringing them in front of you, kind of like the action when making a snow angel. As you finish breathing in your arms should be over your head with the palms facing each other. You are ready for the out breath now.

Now comes the tricky part. As you breathe out, bring your arms down. It should look like you are giving someone a hug. However your hands will be one in front of the other with a gap between them. At this point your right hand should be closest to your face (but not touching it). Your palms are facing in towards your face. Your hands are moving together in line with each other and are not touching. Keep moving your hands down as you continue to breathe out. As you finish your out breath your arms should be fully down.

As you breathe in again let your arms come up your sides. On the next out breath you will want your left hand to be on the inside position and your right hand on the outside position. One must take care to remember to switch the hands during each pass. I find that I end up concentrating on the hand that will next go in front.

Continue the breathing in and breathing out and continue to switch the hands on the inside position. First the right hand, then the left, etc. When you are ready to move on to the next set make sure that the left hand is on the inside.

Second Set - Energy Gathering

As you finish the exhale from the previous movement, and begin your inhale, bring your arms up your sides, palms facing up. Your upper arms will be more or less level with your shoulders and your forearms will be at a forty-five degree angle. You will end up looking like something from Egyptian hieroglyphs. Your arms will stay in this position during the entire movement. During this energy gathering phase, you will be concentrating on your feet.

As you inhale you will pivot your body to the right. Also you will pivot on your right heel turning your right foot to the side. Your left foot will remain facing forward. As you pivot your foot you will also bend both knees so that you are squatting. How deep you squat is up to you, but both knees should be bent.

On the out breath, stand back up, pivot the body to the left. Your right foot will pivot on the heel back to the front and then your left foot pivots on the heel to face the left. Move one foot at a time. Again as you pivot to the left, bend both knees. Repeat moving right to left until you feel ready to move on to the energy movement part. I find that my feet get a heavy feeling during this part.

Second Set - Energy Movement

After exhaling facing the left, inhale, stand up and face the front. While breathing in, your hands will come up outstretched and then push in to the front of your chest, palms facing in, but not touching. It should look like you are about to squeeze a ball together. Your elbows stick out to the sides.

Breathe out and push your hands down to the general level of your groin. Your palms should be facing down. This is the set up for the energy movement set.

To start the movement, turn your palms upward, and as you breathe in, lift your hands upwards until they reach the level of your upper chest or throat, no higher than your shoulders. As you do this you should visualize and feel yourself in a large river flowing upwards.

On the exhale, turn your palms down and push them downwards to your groin. As you do this, visualize and feel yourself in a large river flowing downwards. The upward and downward movements should be deliberate. Repeat these steps as many times as you feel necessary.

When you are ready for the third set you will need to position your hands in a specific way to set up the next set. After an inhale, bringing the hands up to the chest, on the exhale you will leave your left hand where it is, but turn your hand up with the palm facing to the right, kind of like the Shaolin salute. Your right hand will continue to be pushed down to the groin area, palm facing down.

Set Three - Energy Gathering

Now that you are in the starting position, both hands should be curled up into half-closed claw like positions, with the fingers spread a bit apart. During this movement you should be concentrating on your hands. This is the most complex movement and demands exact hand movements. The key is to imagine two upside down L's on the torso. Both start roughly at the collar bone with the long section going down the torso. The short sections move out across the shoulders. The hands will be moving up and down and along these L shaped lines.

It should look something like this:

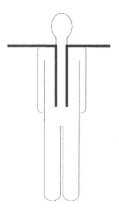

1.   On the inhale, the left hand moves down, with the palms turning down. The right hand moves up the line with the palms turned up. Essentially at this point the hands have merely changed places.

2. On the exhale, the left hand moves back up the line to the original position with the palms turned up. The right hand moves out along the top line out to the right side with the palm turned outwards.

3. On the next inhale, the left hand move to the left along the top

line with the palm turned towards the left. The right hand moves back towards the center with the palm turned towards the left. Essentially on this inhale, both hands are moving towards the left.

4. On the exhale, the left hand returns to the center, with the palm turned towards the right. The right hand moves down with the palm facing down. You have now returned to the original position.

A single repetition is all four above steps and involves two inhales and exhales. When you are ready to move on to the next movement, make sure your hands are in the original position.

Set Three - Energy Movement

This movement is a sweeping, open kind of movement. From the ending position of the previous movement as you breathe in, turn your body

to the right. Unlike the first movement where you only twist at the waist, here you twist at the knees and get your whole body into the movement. The knees should be slightly bent. The hands still retain the claw like shape. As you turn to the right, you rake the air in front of you, the leading hand on top. That is, if you are turning to the right, the right hand is on top.

At the end of this initial movement rotate your hands so the left is on top.

On the exhale, twist your body to the left, again, the left hand should be on top. Really get your whole body into the motion. If your back pops, you are doing it correctly. It is a flowing kind of motion. I like to joke that you should look like you are at a Grateful Dead concert.

Finishing Move

When you are ready to stop, on the inhale, face the front and grab your waist, kind of getting a grip on your love handles. If you don't have any, then pretend. Give an exhale and seal with Tunai. The Qi Gong is complete.

Appendix C
Recommended Reading

Here's a list of books, about runes and other subjects that I recommend for further study.

Taking Up The Runes – Diana Paxson

This is a great book for beginners looking to learn about runes, especially with an eye towards divination. The author not only gives her ideas, but also presents the viewpoints of different authors. This gives a great overview of the runes.

The Rune Primer – Sweyn Plowright

I love this book. Sweyn stresses primary sources and the rune meanings given are very close to my own ideas. It is well balanced and very accessible.

Reading The Past Runes – R.I. Page

This is a must have book if you are studying the runes. It is a purely mundane perspective on the runes, the history, names, etc. The author is actually quite against the idea of runes being used for magic or other supernatural aspects of runes. However, despite this it is good to have a non-esoteric viewpoint of runes.

The Rune Poems

I always recommend going to the primal sources for runes as much as possible. Find yourself some good translations and study them. Try to interpret the various kennings for yourself. Keep going back the rune poems as you read other authors that may get too out there with their speculations.

The Havamal

This is also really good to read especially the latter part that goes over Odin winning the runes. I also believe there are keys to rune use within those sections that still need to be explored.

Bibliography

Aswynn, Freya *The Leaves of Yggdrasil* (St. Paul, Llewellyn Publications, 1994)

Brand, Damon, *Magickal Servitors*, 2016

Gerrard, Katie *Odin's Gateways* (London, BM Avalonia, 2009)

Gerrard, Katie *Seidr: The Gate is Open* (London, MB Avalonia, 2011)

Gundarsson, Kveldulf *Teutonic Magic* (St. Paul, Llewellyn Publications, 1990)

Gundarsson, Kveldulf (editor) *Our Troth, volume 1 History and Lore* (The Troth, 2006)

Kraig, Donald Michael *Modern Magick* (St. Paul, Llewellyn Publications, 1989)

Martin, Coleman, *Communing With The Spirits* (York Beach, Weiser1998)

Tuitéan, Paul *The Roots of Midgard* (Self Published, 1995)

Page, R.I. *Reading the Past Runes* (Berkley, University of California Press, 1993)

Paxson, Diana *Taking Up The Runes* (Boston, Weiser, 2005)

Sibley, Jane Ph.d *Some Notes on Rune Use, Norse Traditional Magic, and Runic Divination* (Self Published, 1994)

Sibley, Jane Pd.d *The Divine Thunderbolt* (Xlibris, 2009)

Thorsson, Edred *Futhark* (York Beach, Weiser, 1984)

Thorsson, Edred *Runelore* (York Beach, Weiser, 1987)

Thorsson, Edred *At The Well of Wyrd* (York Beach, Weiser, 1993)

Thorsson, Örnólfur (editor) *The Sagas of Icelanders* (New York, Penguin Putnam, 2000)

Index

Made in the USA
Coppell, TX
09 December 2023

25714835R00177